Introduction

"Sixty Years of Changes in Major League Baseball"

There have been more significant changes in Major League Baseball in the past 60 years than there were since the inception of the game. The changes we will be looking at did not occur all at once, but were rather an evolutionary process. The years following the end of the Second World War helped America become the most successful and powerful nation the world has ever known. In 1947, the population of the United States was 145,124,000, with a life expectancy of 66.8 years. By 2009, the population had grown to 305,529,000 with a life expectancy of 77.9 years. Demographic trends describe the changes in populations over time. These changes and the expansion of our country created a desire to grow Major League Baseball. Baseball was happy to meet this need by issuing franchises to teams that met certain requirements. After World War II, there were four major forces that changed America. Let's look at each of these in greater detail and how they affected baseball.

1. **Television**

By 1939, America had become aware that there was something new and wonderful about to become a reality. At the 1939 World's Fair in New York City, there was a demonstration of a new device that would revolutionize the dissemination of information in American homes. To many it seemed like something out of a Buck Roger's science fiction comic book. Public availability of television would take a number of years to develop. The technology presented was still in its infancy. The networks and the methods of carrying the signals such as laying co-axial cables were yet to be developed. When the war came in 1941, most television stations suspended operations until the war ended. It was not until 1947, that the television industry and America's insatiable hunger to be entertained would merge into reality. That reality would change America forever. In what way did television change America? This is a difficult question because it has so many answers. It has certainly opened our understanding of the world in which we live. It teaches us. It entertains us. It educates us. It brings into our lives, events and places of the world we would never have imagined. It brings drama, music and culture. It is the window to the world. It is America's source of information and it causes us to form opinions and to think. I hope you understand that the full impact television has brought to America and to the world cannot be measured. The few remarks I have made about the impact of television on America and the world is so minute, that it is comparable to putting one's toe into the ocean.

2. **The G.I. Bill** (Readjustment Act of 1944)

Over 16 million young men and women served

in the Second World War period. They went in as boys and girls and came out as strong men and women. They had been tried and tested and knew exactly what they wanted for their lives when they returned. To answer their desire, a grateful nation gave them a precious gift, the gift of education. After going through the Great Depression and the Second World War, only a small percentage of these veterans would have ever gone to college had it not been for the G.I. Bill. Not only did the bill help with tuition and books, but it also provided loan guarantees for homes, farms and businesses. In 1947, 49% of those enrolled in colleges were veterans. From this generation came our doctors, our teachers, our engineers and attorneys, plus a great variety of other skilled workers who were necessary in the development of our nation. America was getting educated as never before.

3. **Commercial Jet Aviation**

Prior to and during World War II, design and development of jet aviation was exclusively focused on the military. After all, winning the war was of paramount importance. After the war, commercial jet aviation was slow in developing. Other countries took the lead, while America took a wait and see approach. It was not as simple as taking an existing plane and putting a jet engine into it. There were enormous engineering challenges to be overcome. New metal alloys had to be developed. New airframes (that is the entire plane) had to be designed from scratch. In short, an entirely new industry had to be developed with only the experience of World War

II technology to guide them. Jet engines would create more thrust and require less maintenance than the piston engine planes. They also used a great deal more fuel, which added to the cost. Jet planes flew faster and higher, were more efficient over long flights and would fly at up to 550 miles an hour at altitudes of up to 49,000 feet. Jet planes accelerated more slowly than propeller planes and required longer runways so airports had to be redesigned.

Later in 1959, and early into the 1960s, commercial airlines began to provide scheduled domestic flights. Transworld Airlines (TWA) and United Airlines (UA) were among the early companies providing jet service. Other airlines here and abroad followed, providing regularly scheduled commercial jet service. The leading manufacturers for jet planes were Douglas and Boeing. This was the first time in our history that America was united by jet aviation from coast-to-coast. Just think about it, a businessman could fly from New York to Denver, Colorado, take care of his business and fly back to New York in the same day. The same trip could have taken up to four days by train. We shall see that jet aviation would help in the expansion of Major League Baseball from coast to coast.

4. **The Federal Highway Act of 1956.**

The fourth great event that changed America was the enactment of the Federal Highway Act of 1956 under President Eisenhower's administration. It was the largest public works project in the history of our nation. This Act created a network of superhighways that connected the major population centers of America. Major shifts in population can be directly traced to this Act. To take a phrase from Kevin Costner's movie Field of Dreams, "If you build it, they will come". There could not have been any more truth for this time period than there is in this statement. People and populations followed the roads. Commercial jet aviation played a major role in the expansion and development of our country, but the Highway Act of 1956 was a force that developed the country from within. The impact of which, is impossible to measure. Just think of what affect it had on the automobile industry alone. Americans could drive reliable cars over these wonderful highways to multiple destinations in a relatively short amount of time with greater safety and comfort. They could go places and see things they only dreamed about before. It seems important to those reading this book to understand the forces that have caused America to expand and grow. Obviously there were other events that contributed to America's growth; however, I believe these four forces: television, the G.I. Bill, commercial jet aviation and the Highway Act of 1956 had the greatest impact on America.

As we begin to look into the changes in baseball, perhaps the reader will have a greater understanding of how these forces changed America and at the same time had a considerable impact on the game of baseball as well.

Table of Contents

Table of Contents

Jackie Robinson

CHAPTER

Breaking the Color Barrier

Prior to 1946, Major League Baseball had not changed in any appreciable way since the beginning of the 1900s. There were eight teams in each of the two leagues, the American League and the National League. They played a 154 game schedule. The team in each league with the highest percentage of wins versus losses was named that league's champion. The winner of each league would then play a best of seven games World Series. The winner of the Series was then declared baseball's world champion.

There were two distinct characteristics in baseball at that time. First, was that all Major League games were played east of the Mississippi River. The St. Louis Cardinals and the St. Louis Browns were the farthest westerly teams. Second, all Major League baseball players were white.

Through the foresight and wisdom of Branch Rickey of the Brooklyn Dodgers and the bravery and skills of Jackie Robinson, baseball was soon to be open to all races. The color barrier would finally be broken. In 1946, Jackie Robinson signed a Major League contract for $600 per month. He was assigned to the Brooklyn Dodgers AAA affiliate, the Montréal Royals in the International League, where he played all through the year of 1946. The following year, he was brought up to the Brooklyn Dodgers and became the first black American to play in the Major Leagues. This was a great victory for baseball and a greater victory for America. To understand how deeply the color barrier was ingrained into the America psyche, please consider that at the height of the second world war, up until 1943, the armed forces were still segregated.

It was not going to be easy for Robinson and he knew it. The story is told, that before the 1947 season began, Branch Rickey had Jackie Robinson come into his office and explained to him how difficult it was going to be. He went into great detail about what Robinson was going to encounter. He said, "They are going to say the vilest things imaginable about you, your mother and your family and anybody associated with you." There are those that do not want you to be in the big leagues. Robinson asked Mr. Ricky, "Do you want a Negro who is afraid to fight back?" Mr. Ricky answered and said, "We know you can play ball and we want a ballplayer with the guts not to fight back. You're going to do the job with hits, stolen bases and fielding ground balls, and nothing else." Mr. Ricky made an agreement with Jackie that he would not retaliate in any way for any bad treatment he would receive for three years. Jackie agreed.

When Robinson joined the Brooklyn Dodgers, there were players on the team who said they would refuse to play if Robinson was on the team. Dixie Walker was one of the leading opponents against having Robinson on the team. However, Pee-wee Reese became the peacemaker. The problem was never completely resolved, but they did get on with the baseball season. There were other teams in the league that said that they would refuse to play against the Brooklyn Dodgers if Robinson was in the lineup. The Commissioner of baseball said that if any player refused to play because of Jackie Robinson, he would be suspended.

To give you an idea of how deep the color barrier ran, I would like to relate a story that actually happened. On one occasion in 1947, Brooklyn was playing the St. Louis Cardinals. Jackie Robinson was at that time playing first base and Enos "Country" Slaughter was at bat. Slaughter hit a ground ball to shortstop and Jackie took the throw at first base. Instead of going for first base, Slaughter jumped into the lower leg of Robinson and spiked him, causing him to have a number of stitches to close the wound. Robinson never retaliated. After the three year period was up, Brooklyn was again playing the St Louis Cardinals and Enos Slaughter was on first base after having gotten a base hit. Jackie Robinson was playing second base at the time. The next hitter hit a ball to the shortstop and threw the ball to Robinson for a routine double-play. Instead of throwing the ball to first base, Robinson threw it at Slaughter, right in the mouth and knocked out several teeth. Enos Slaughter never said a word.

Jackie Robinson was one of the most exciting, dynamic baseball players ever to play the game. Because of his speed and daring, he drove other pitchers crazy when he got on base. They did not know if he was going to steal 2nd, 3rd or home. The other players of the opposing team also had problems with Jackie because of his daring running skills.

You may remember the photograph of Jackie Robinson stealing home plate against the Yankees in the 1955 World Series. Jackie was on 3rd base and he made several fake starts to steal home plate but always went back to 3rd base. On the 4th attempt, he went straight for the plate. Yogi Berra claims to this day that Robinson was out but high speed photos showed that Robinson was in fact safe. What is utterly amazing is the fact that Jackie Robinson stole home plate 19 times during his career. It almost boggles the mind to realize how good he really was. Jackie's final game was September 30, 1956. He was inducted into the Baseball Hall Of Fame in 1962. Major League Baseball has designated April 15 as Jackie Robinson Day to honor and commemorate what he meant to baseball and the country. All uniformed players in both leagues wear Number 42 (Jackie's number) in his honor.

After Robinson came into the Big Leagues in 1947, other black players followed. The St. Louis Browns brought up Hank Thompson on July 17, 1947 and Willard Brown on August 17, 1947. Other black players from the Negro Leagues would also become Major League Baseball players. Larry Doby would sign with the Cleveland Indians and Luke Easter also signed and eventually the ageless one, Satchel Paige also became a Major League Baseball player.

Jackie's Early Life

Jackie Robinson was born in 1919 in Cairo, Georgia. His mother and his siblings moved to Pasadena, Ca in 1920 to live with relatives. She had hoped that conditions there would be better than they were in Georgia. From a racial standpoint, they were not. Jackie went to Muir Technical School. After graduation, he attended the University of California and excelled in baseball, football and basketball. Robinson joined the army in 1942 and was honorably discharged in 1944. After that he played for a short time in the Negro Leagues before signing with the Brooklyn Dodgers.

He played with the Brooklyn Dodgers from 1947 to 1956. He entered the big leagues later in life. He was 28 years old when he started his major league career.

After baseball retirement, Jackie Robinson joined Chock Full of Nuts Coffee Company and was made vice president and director of personnel. This made Jackie exceedingly happy.

Jackie Robinson won the Rookie of the Year Award his first year in the big leagues. Two years later, he was voted the National League's most valuable player. It could be argued that Jackie

Robinson's entry into the big leagues in 1947 did more for race relations in the United states than it did for baseball. After a 16 year career, Robinson retired on January 5, 1957. After suffering the ravages of diabetes, he died on October 24, 1972 at the age of 53.

Through the bravery and skill of Jackie Robinson and the foresight and determination of Branch Rickey, the door was opened wide and baseball would never again have the stain of segregation attached to it.

Through the courtesy of the University of Central Florida (UCF), the Department of Diversity and Ethics headed by Professor Richard E. Lapchick, the following is the ethics diversity statistics in Major League Baseball for 2009:
1. 59.9% white
2. 8.5% Black Americans
3. 28.7% Latinos
4. 2.5% Asians
5. 27.4% of the players in the Big Leagues in 2009 were born outside of the United States.

CHAPTER

The Reserve Clause

In the late 19th Century, baseball became popular enough that people would pay money to watch teams of players compete. As a result, the owners were fearful that the good players would go to other teams to attain higher salaries and that the other teams would be eager to sign them. To combat this, the owners conspired among themselves and promulgated a standard one-year contract that contained what came to be known as the Reserve Clause.

This meant that once a player signed this contract, he was bound to that team indefinitely. The player was not free to enter into any subsequent contract with any other team. The only way a player could be free of the contract was to be released by the original team or traded. All contracts were for one year and were renegotiated for salary each year. Players became accustomed to the fact that their salary was based on whether or not they had a good year, a mediocre year or a poor year. If they had a good year, they could ask for a raise. If they had a bad year, they might be subjected to a cut in pay. They could negotiate their contracts; however, if the offer the owners made was the final offer, they were bound to accept the contract or not play at all.

There is a story that is told about Babe Ruth. When a reporter asked him how he felt to be making more money than the President of the United States, he replied, "I had a better year than he did".

The owners also colluded regarding the trading of players. They decided they would not trade certain players and the other teams agreed. This was strictly a monopoly. The Reserve Clause was by all logical standards a monopoly violating the Sherman Anti-Trust Act. Each time the law was tested, the courts held in favor of the owners and against the players. Plus, the United States Supreme Court had held in the 1922 case, Federal Baseball versus National League, that baseball was an amusement and that organizing a schedule of games between independent owners and operating clubs in various states and engaging in activities incidental thereto did not constitute interstate commerce and therefore the antitrust laws did not apply to such activities.

There came a glimmer of hope on December 24, 1969, when a player named Curt Flood challenged the reserve clause. Flood had been a 12 year veteran of the St. Louis Cardinals and had been nominated three times to the All-Star roster of the National League. The Cardinals informed Flood that he was going to be traded to the Philadelphia Phillies. Flood did not want to be traded and wrote a letter to baseball commissioner Bowie Kuhne, which read

Curt Flood

as follows. "After 12 years in the major leagues, I do not feel that I am a piece of property to be bought or sold, irrespective of my wishes." He wanted to play in 1970 for the Cardinals and wanted to consider other offers. Kuhne denied his request. Flood sued Commissioner Kuhne and Major League Baseball.

The case went all the way to the Federal Supreme Court. The court held in favor of Major League Baseball in a 5 to 3 decision. Although Flood lost the battle, he didn't lose the war. He paved the way for the final destruction of the Reserve Clause. In 1974, Charlie Finley, who was the owner of the Oakland Athletics made an error in his contract payment to Catfish Hunter. He was supposed to have made a $50,000 payment to an annuity set up in Hunter's contract. Instead, he paid the $50,000 directly to Hunter which violated his contract. A federal arbitrator granted Hunter free agency. Thus Catfish Hunter became the major leagues' first free agent, after which he signed a lucrative contract with the New York Yankees. He went on to have a very successful Major League career culminating in his induction into the Baseball Hall of Fame.

Charley Finley moved the Athletics from Kansas City to Oakland California in 1968. On May 8th 1968 in a game against the Minnesota Twins, Hunter pitched the first perfect game in the American League since 1922. He continued to win games. In 1974, Hunter received the Cy Young Award and was named Pitcher of the Year by the Sporting News. Hunter's statistics while he was with the Athletics were impressive. He had 4 consecutive years with at least 20 wins, 4 World Series wins and no loses.

When Hunter was granted free agency, and signed with the New York Yankees, his contract with the New York Yankees in 1975 made him the highest paid pitcher in baseball. That year Hunter had a 20 game winning season again. He also lead the Yankees to 3 straight pendants from 1976 to 1979.

The effects of diabetes began to tell on the pitcher. In 1979 at age 33, Catfish Hunter retired from baseball. In 1987, he was inducted into the National Baseball Hall of Fame. A few years after his retirement, he was diagnosed with ALS, Lou Gehrig's disease. On September 9th 1999 Catfish Hunter died of ALS.

It is truly an unusual circumstance that both Lou Gehrig and Jim Catfish Hunter would die of ALS and both play for the New York Yankees.

In 1975, a federal arbitrator, Peter Seitz decided that since Andy Messerschmitt and Dave McNally had played one season without a contract, they could become free agents. This decision essentially dismantled the reserve clause and opened the door to widespread free agency. This decision was monumental. It drove a stake into the black heart of the reserve clause that had enslaved baseball players for over 70 years. There was one caveat, however, where a vestige of the reserve clause still remains. That was the fact that when a player opted for free agency, he agreed that he would stay with the club that purchased his contract for six years. The rationale behind this was the fact that the purchasing club felt that it would take that long to recoup their initial investment in the player being acquired.

The inglorious history of the reserve clause had finally come to an end and with the advent of free agents baseball had entered a new era.

CHAPTER

Minor League Baseball

Minor league baseball has had a rich heritage in America since its inception in 1902. On September 5, 1901, five owners met in Chicago to form the National Association of Professional Baseball Leagues. They started with 14 leagues and 96 teams for the 1902 season. Patrick T. Powers was named as the first president. When he left office in 1909, there were 35 leagues and 246 teams. Marshall Sexton succeeded him and served until 1932. In his first few years, Marshall had to battle the outlawed federal league and Major League Baseball which were raiding his top players . It might be emphasized that the National Association of Baseball Leagues was not under the heinous control of the reserve clause as was Major League Baseball, and that it retained its name until it was changed in 1999 to the "Minor Leagues".

In 1921, Branch Rickey, then general manager of the St. Louis Cardinals, conceived the idea of having major league teams own minor league teams to have what he termed a farm system to feed players into the big leagues after they were developed. By 1929, three other teams had similar affiliations and by the end of the next decade, all 16 teams had made similar arrangements. This was of course a great blow to minor league baseball as Major League Baseball had the ability to include a reserve clause in the contracts of minor league baseball players.

At the height of its operation, Branch Rickey's farm system controlled 32 minor league teams with approximately 600 players. Baseball Commissioner, Kenesaw Mountain Landis was concerned that Mr. Rickey controlled too large a percentage of the minor league baseball players. As a result, he made him release 70 players. This however, did not deter Mr. Rickey from going ahead with his farm system. Branch Rickey was the greatest innovator baseball had ever seen. Aside from breaking the color barrier by bringing Jackie Robinson into the big leagues in 1947, his innovations became fixtures in our national pastime. Although he may not have known it when he was building his farm system, he may have saved our present minor league system.

At the end of World War II, starting in 1945, minor league baseball expanded rapidly all over the country. The peak came in 1949 when minor league attendance reached 39.7 million fans. There were 59 leagues and 450 teams. It seemed as if every small town in the United States had a minor league baseball team. There were more classifications at that time than there are today. D ball was the lowest baseball team classification with C, B, A, AA and AAA the highest.

Even earlier, the minor leagues were popular all over the United States. Many minor league teams flourished in the 30's and 40's. To name a few: there was the Pacific Coast League, the International League and the American Association which were all AAA leagues, the Texas League (AA), "Sally" League (A), Carolina League (B), Western Association (C), and Florida State League (D).

Minor league baseball can be credited with one of the greatest innovations in the game night baseball. In 1930, in the Western League's Des Moines, Iowa team played Wichita, Kansas, under the lights. This idea spread rapidly, helping the minor leagues during the Great Depression and eventually making it into the big leagues. Night baseball revolutionized the industry like nothing ever had. Can you imagine that until 1930, all baseball, (major and minor leagues), was played in the daytime. The Chicago Cubs were the last holdout, putting lighting into Wrigley Field on August 8, 1988.

I mentioned earlier that Branch Rickey was responsible for saving minor league baseball. If he had not instituted the program where Major League teams could own or have working agreements with minor league teams, all of minor league baseball would have perished, for, with Major League Baseball readily available on television, interest in the minors faded.

Today all Major League clubs have between seven and nine minor league teams mainly in the upper classes - A, AA, AAA and some of the rookie leagues, formerly class D. The Class D, C, and B leagues did not survive. The leagues that have gone into history were popular names like the Three I League, the Carolina League, and the New England League. America can look back before television and remember the joy that minor-league baseball brought to many small towns in this country.

From personal experience, I can tell you it was a happy time. In 1947, while playing in the Ohio State League Class D ball in Marion Ohio. I had a wonderful, moving experience happen to me that year. Two days before the start of the season, the city had a baseball banquet with many dignitaries attending. They were all seated at the head table. There was an elderly man seated in the last seat to the right. I found out later he was 80 years of age. All the ball players got up and began to introduce themselves to the men at the front table. I went up to the elderly man and said my name is Jim Forbes and he said mine is Cy Young. I could not believe that I was shaking hands with the most famous pitcher that ever lived, having won 511 games. Cy Young was born in Gilmore, Ohio March 29, 1867. He was elected to the Baseball Hall Of Fame in 1937. Not only had he won 511 games in a 22 year career. Major League Baseball memorialized Cy Young's achievements in pitching by an award given yearly to the best pitcher in each league. This award is called the Cy Young Award. It was truly a memorable experience to meet such a baseball legend.

In 1947 Marion, Ohio was a town of 27,000 people with 70 home games, we drew in 115,000 fans for an average of 1,550 per game. That little town treated us like kings. If one of us hit the winning run in, the fans would pass the hat and when we left the field they handed us a handful of dollars. The ballpark was part of a larger city park. We sometimes played split doubleheaders, one game at one o'clock and one game at seven o'clock. Between games many families would get together and prepare a buffet that was fit for a king for the ballplayers. There were restaurants in town that would have the entire ball club out for dinner. Anything you wanted to eat and drink was paid for by the restaurant and they would do this two or three times during the season. It was a happy time for families to enjoy baseball and I really believe it brought the communities closer together.

They also have the baseball draft which I call the college draft. Baseball is somewhat different than the other major sports such as basketball and football. The National Basketball Association and the National Football League do not have farm systems. They don't need them. They have the best farm system in the world. High schools and colleges are their farm system.

Take for example a promising young high school athlete who has great ability and a good physique. He will play about three and a half to four years of high school ball and have good coaching. If he is fortunate enough to get a college scholarship, he will play four years under very good coaching. At the time of the draft if he is chosen high on the list, he will make a great deal of money with a strong possibility that he will play in the NBA or the NFL upon graduation.

In baseball, if a player is chosen high in the draft, he will also make a great deal of money, but he will probably go directly to one of the teams with minor league affiliates, most likely AA. He will then spend time in the minor leagues to learn his craft. He may be invited to spring training with the Major League club to be reevaluated. Depending on his progress, in time he may be brought up to the major leagues. Some players move quickly. For others, it takes several years. Still others never make it. With the exception of pitchers, position players have to pass the acid test. What is the acid test? *The answer is* hitting big league pitching. Some can, but most cannot.

I thought it would be of interest to the readers to understand what an important roll minor-league baseball played in the development of our country. It was a wonderful time for families in this country to see professional baseball players in their own communities. I will never forget the great memories that I enjoyed playing and managing in the minor leagues. Minor league baseball had a special place in American history until it was almost wiped out when television came into *its* prominence in the 1960s.

CHAPTER

Relocation, Expansion and Realignment

The shifts in population resulting from the four profound changes discussed in the introduction caused baseball to adapt to these changes by the relocation of existing franchises and the awarding of new ones. The realignment of each league into divisions ushered in the playoffs system we have today. The following is an outline of relocation and expansion.

In 1953, the Boston Braves moved to Milwaukee and became the Milwaukee Braves. This was the first relocation in 50 years. In 1954, the St. Louis Browns moved to Baltimore and became the Orioles. Prior to that, Baltimore had been in the International League Class AAA (although it had had major league teams early in the 20th Century). The relocations that garnered the most attention took place in 1957 when the Brooklyn Dodgers and the New York Giants moved to the West Coast. Many a heart was broken to see "Dem Bums" move from their beloved Ebbets Field and the Giants from the Polo grounds to Los Angeles and San Francisco, respectively.

Then in 1961, the Washington Senators moved
to Minneapolis St. Paul and became the Minnesota
Twins. To assuage the loss to the baseball fans in
the nation's capital, a franchise was granted, also
to be called the Washington Senators. In 1966, the
Milwaukee Braves moved to Atlanta. In 1968,
Kansas City, which formerly was a Philadelphia
team, moved to Oakland and became the Oakland
Athletics.

In 1970, the Seattle Pilots moved to Milwaukee
and became the Milwaukee Brewers. The Toronto
Blue Jays entered the American League in 1977. In
1972, the second Washington Senators moved to
Arlington Texas and became the Texas Rangers. In
1993, two more franchises were granted; the
Colorado Rockies and the Florida Marlins. In 2005,
the Montréal Expos moved to Washington, D.C. and
became the Washington Nationals. The last two
franchises to be granted went to the Tampa Bay
Devil Rays and the Arizona Diamondbacks. This
completed the transition from 16 teams to 30 teams.
It took 45 years - from 1953 to 1998 to accomplish
this transition. It would be remiss of me if I did not
mention one the the major changes in major league
baseball since it began. In 1961 the American League
expanded to 10 teams and their schedule went from
154 games to 162 games. When the National League
expanded to 10 teams in 1962, it also went to the
162 game schedule.

Essentially this addition changed baseball into
2 eras, the historic era and the modern era.

Henceforth it would be impossible to compare the accomplishments of the players in the historic era with that of the players in the modern era. It will always be argued whether or not Roger Maris really broke Babe Ruth's record of 60 home runs. Babe hit his 60th home run in the 154th game. Maris hit his 61st home run on the 162nd game. Babe would have had 8 more games and maybe 25 more times at bat. Ater all, he did hit 17 home runs in the month of September. We will never know the answer to this question.

There will be many *ifs and buts* about the 2 eras, but as Don Meridith the great quarterback for the Dallas Cowboys and sports announcer said "If *ifs and buts* were fruits and nuts, we all would have a wonderful time at Christmas." There will be many *ifs and buts* about the 2 eras.

Regardless of the comparisons, the historic era will always be the game your fathers watched.

Don Meredith along with Frank Gifford and Howard Cosell brought us the 1st televised Monday night football game. Gifford did the play by play and kept Meredith and Cosell from the barbs they fired at each other but it was all good fun.

Realignment

Here is how it worked: There are still only two leagues, the American and the National, but we now have 30 teams instead of only the 16 prior to the expansion. Each league has three divisions: East, Central and West. The American League has 14 teams and the National League has 16 teams. Looking logically at this, one might ask why not 15 teams in each league? It seems that there would have been a scheduling problem and at present, the 14/16 team arrangement seems to work best. The playoffs operate as follows. Each division leader enters into the playoffs. That would mean there would be only three teams in each league competing against each other in the playoffs, which would again cause an imbalance. To solve this problem, a fourth team was needed in each league to make the playoffs even, at four teams each. Thus, they created the wild card team. The wild card team was selected as the team, other than the division leaders, who had the best win and loss percentage. If there were a tie, it would be decided by a one game playoff. The playoffs begin with the four teams in each league playing off in a best of 3 out of 5 series to determine who goes on to play in the league championship series. This is a best four games out of seven series playoff. The National League Champion and the America League Champion meet in the World Series, which is decided by a best four out of seven series.

The winner of the World Series is declared Baseball's World Champion.

Divisions of the American League and the National League

American League

East

Baltimore Orioles
Boston Red Sox
New York Yankees
Tampa Bay Rays
Toronto Blue Jays

Central

Chicago White Sox
Cleveland Indians
Detroit Tigers
Kansas City Royals
Minnesota Twins

West

Los Angeles Angels
Oakland Athletics
Texas Rangers
Seattle Mariners

National League

East

Atlanta Braves
Florida Marlins
New York Mets
Philadelphia Phillies
Washington Nationals

Central

Chicago Cubs
Cincinnati Reds
Houston Astros
Milwaukee Brewers
Pittsburgh Pirates
St Louis Cardinals

West

Arizona Diamondbacks
Los Angeles Dodgers
San Diego Padres
San Francisco Giants
Colorado Rockies

Interleague Play

In addition to the playoffs system, the next big innovation in baseball was interleague play. There were many reasons to have interleague play. The 1994, 1995 calamitous strike, turned many fans away from baseball. The inauguration of interleague play was to peak the fans interest in baseball and bring them back to the game. Teams in each league would play each other. Interleague play started June 12, 1997.

Starting in 2002, the National League Divisions began playing against the American League Divisions. The American League East played the National League West. The American League Central played the National League East. The American League West played the National League Central. Popular match-ups prior to this format were the New York Yankees versus the New York Mets and the Chicago Cubs verses the Chicago White Sox. These two match-ups were preserved. The format of division play mentioned above is expected to continue, since interleague plan became very popular with the fans. The designated hitter rule would apply when teams played in American League cities but not in National League cities.

CHAPTER

The Players Union

In the late 1800s and early 1900s, there had been several attempts to unionize professional baseball. They were the formation of the Brotherhood of Professional Players in 1885, the Players Protection Association in 1900, the Fraternity of Professional Players of America in 1912, and the National Baseball Players Association of the United States in 1922. None of these groups were successful in securing concessions from baseball's ownership and were ultimately dissolved.

After the 1919 baseball scandal, where members of the Chicago White Sox accepted money to throw the World Series, baseball hired its first commissioner. He was a former judge by the name of Kennesaw Mountain Landis. He had white, flowing wild hair with chiseled features that gave him a fearsome look of authority. He ruled with an iron fist and woe to the person that was on the receiving end of his wrath. His job was to clean up baseball and bring credibility back to the game. Commissioner Landis was hired by the owners of baseball and was backed up by the reserve clause which he enforced vigorously. The players had no appeal process, no arbitrator, no one to hear their complaints. When they did take their concerns to the courts, the courts invariably ruled in favor of the owners. As you can see from this, baseball was a very one-sided situation—all in favor of the owners.

The Major League Baseball Players Association was created in 1953. It was the first time since 1922 that major League Baseball players were able to organize into a powerful labor union. The primary function of any labor union is to get the best salaries and other benefits that they can in a collective bargaining agreement with management. The Major League Baseball Players Association has done their job extremely well. In 1966, the union hired Marvin Miller from the United Steel Workers of America to serve as Executive Director. There had long been a need for major league players to unite as a union to fight against the many abuses that had been heaped upon them for over 100 years by the owners and the reserve clause. In 1968, Miller negotiated the first collective bargaining agreement with the club owners which also included arbitration over salary disputes.

The success of that changed major sports for ever, thanks to Miller. Many milestones were reached—salaries, pension funds, licensing rights and revenues were brought to new levels. The players union became one of the strongest labor unions in the country, bringing with it great leverage through player strikes and the ever present threat of strikes. There have been eight work stoppages, five player strikes and three owner lockouts.

Don Fear, a Kansas City attorney assisted Marvin Miller until 1986, when he became executive director. This was a period of unprecedented growth in which industry revenues climbed to over $1 billion. Player salaries went from an average of $413,000 in 1986, to slightly over $3 million in 2009.

The 1994-1995 strike was the worst in Major League history. There were attempts by management to break the unions and to implement pay cuts and reductions in pension benefits. The 1994-1995 strike lasted from August 12, 1994 to April 2, 1995. The 232 day strike caused the cancellation of over 900 games, including all of the postseason. As a result, there was no 1994 World Series, and this was the first cancellation of a World Series since 1904. The 1995 season was also shortened because of the length of the strike. A collective bargaining agreement was signed with management which runs through 2011. There has been sixteen years of the labor peace and hopefully this will continue.

There is no question that Major League players benefited enormously under Miller and Fear. The owners, individually or collectively were forced to significantly share their revenues with the players for the first time since the game began.

We have talked about the players, the unions, and the owners, but what about the baseball fan? Where did he fit into this equation? Baseball may do many strange things, but one thing especially dangerous to do is to cancel a World Series. It is almost as bad as canceling Christmas.

Let's face it, the fans didn't care who had the strongest case in the strike. They didn't care who was right or wrong. All they saw was a bunch of money grubbing people fighting for their point of view and using the American people as the leverage to accomplish their objectives.

What about the guy who has put down his hard earned money to buy tickets for himself and his family to the ballgame? The guy drinks the beer, eats the hot dogs, and pays increased cable bills to watch these millionaires play baseball. What about his rights?

When the strike was finally over, the message went out loud and clear. Attendance all over Major League Baseball dropped like a rock. One said, "If they care more about the money than they do about the fans, let them keep it all". Some returned; others never did. One man in a large city rented a small plane pulling a banner with a sign on it, which read, you can all go to . . . (name the place that is very warm and it was not Florida).

Most fans eventually came back and you know what brought them back? It was the steroid era—another scandal. A time when Sammy Sosa, Mark McGuire and Barry Bonds were hitting baseballs out of ballparks with great regularity. Who knew about it?—the unions, the owners and the players.

They all knew about it. The owners loved it; more fans in the seats, more beer sold, more hot dogs, and happy days are here again, but for the next five to seven years, management paid a high price for this outrage, as will be detailed in the next chapter.

The union was also instrumental in challenging the reserve clause. As noted previously, the reserve clause was never eliminated in a court of law, but it was struck down by an independent arbitrator in 1975. The union helped to achieve this ruling, which won the players the right to free agency.

CHAPTER

Television and Baseball

In the introduction, we discussed the role that television had played in the growth of America after the second world war. Now we will focus our attention specifically on how television and baseball have benefited each other. Major-league baseball and the television industry have been one of the most profitable business marriages the country has ever known. Each has contributed to the enormous prosperity of the other, the profits of which have run into the billions of dollars.

Prior to the advent of television, the only way a person could see Major League ball players was to go to a ballpark. That is of course, if you lived in one of the big cities east of the Mississippi River. The first televised Major League game was played on August 26, 1939, on station W-2 X 85, which would become WNBC TV, Channel 4 in New York. Red Barber was the announcer and the game was played between the Cincinnati Reds and the Brooklyn Dodgers at Ebbets Field in Brooklyn, New York. At the 1939 World's Fair in New York City, America became aware of television. Television was the primary featured exhibit and organizers believed that the Dodgers/Reds double-header on August 26 was the perfect event to showcase the new technology. Television technology was in its infancy, and, with the advent of the second world war, all television broadcasting companies suspended operations till after the war.

In the early 1950's, some bars and saloons had television sets to attract customers where one could watch other sporting events like Gillette's Friday night fights or one or two variety shows. By the mid-1950's, a high percentage of the homes in America had television sets. They generally had 7- or 11-inch screens with a rooftop or an inside antenna called rabbit ears. These rabbit ears were about 12 to 24 inches long and could be swiveled to pick up the television signal at its strongest point. Rooftop antennas gave much better reception and, for about $10-$12, one could purchase a rooftop antenna kit at a local hardware store. If you and your neighbor were brave enough to get onto the roof to install the antenna and attach the wiring, your television set would provide a better picture. Some neighborhood roofs were such a mass of these ugly contraptions that they resembled something out of a horror movie. It seemed as though a metal forest had sprung up before our eyes.

In 1946, the New York Yankees became the first team with a local television contract when it sold the rights of their games for $75,000. By the end of the century, the *same* rights were sold for $52 million per season. By 1951, the World Series was a television standard. By 1956, all teams sold at the least some of their games to local television stations. Bear in mind that these financial agreements were made long before baseball expansion began. In 1966, Major League Baseball followed the lead of the National Football League and sold its first league-wide national television package netting $300,000 per team. The latest national television contract paid 24 million to each team in 2002.

The following is a table showing the calculations of total television revenue, average ticket prices and average players' salary from 1964 to 2002 (at five year intervals):

Total TV Revenue/Avg. Ticket Prices/Avg. Players Salaries		
1964:	21.28(M)	13.01	85, 907
1969:	38.04(M)	12.76	121,796
1974:	43.25(M)	11.25	148,248
2001:		17.96	2,378,803
2002:		17.85	2,385,903

Note: This is 1989 and 1992 national television data only. No local television data is included.

The chart and certain other data have been provided by the courtesy of the Professor of Economics at the University of Wisconsin at La Crosse, Michael J. Haupert.   Professor Haupert's recent study on the economic history of baseball is an excellent source of information about our national pastime.

The above chart emphasizes most vividly the tremendous impact television has had on Major League Baseball. The introduction of cable, pay-per-view and other satellite communications has also increased revenues. In addition, technology has made tremendous strides in bringing the television viewer an awesome array of images, angles, and replays which seem to bring the game right into one's living room.

Television and baseball have come a long way and the marriage has been very successful. In 1947, the average big-league player's salary was $11,000 per year.   In 2009, it reached the staggering $3 million mark.   Obviously, other factors, such as collective bargaining agreements between the players union and management, played a significant role in the player salary. However, the television industry was a driving force that brought baseball into the homes of the American people and is certainly responsible for the high incomes that players enjoy today.

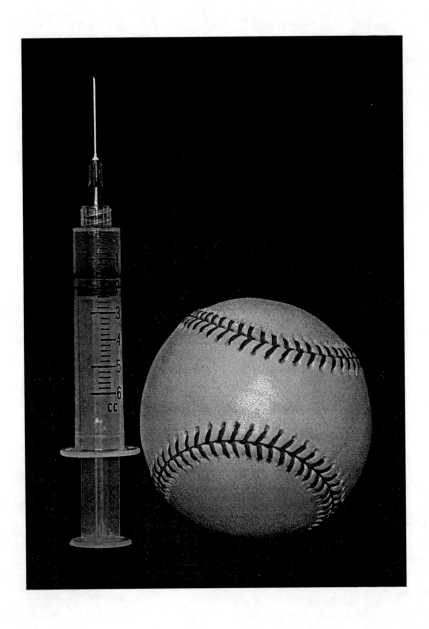

CHAPTER

Baseball's Steroid Era

In the history of competitive sports, athletes have sometimes attempted to gain an advantage by taking performance enhancing substances. We have seen the tragedy of this play out in the Olympic Games, long before it became evident in baseball. In 1988, a Canadian runner named Ben Johnson ran the fastest 100 meters in history. Shortly thereafter, he tested positive for illegal substances and was immediately suspended and later banned. The international Olympic style drug testing has been most effective and the model for all other sports testing. Athletes are tested before each event such as the Tour de France, under rules established by the World Anti-Doping Agency.

It is interesting to note, that even in thoroughbred racing, horses are tested after each race. The steward, who is responsible for enforcing the rules of racing, selects certain horses to be tested. Not all horses are tested; the choices are based on the protocol set up by the rules of racing for past performances. Some are tested when they perform poorly in a race where historically they have performed better; conversely, some are tested when they perform better in a race where they have historically done poorly.

Baseball was slow in taking action to combat this growing problem. Awareness regarding growth hormones has gradually increased ever since they were successfully synthesized by Dr. Choh Huo Li at the University of California in San Francisco in 1971 where he was a biochemist and the director of Molecular Endocrinology. There are several types of growth hormones available in the United States and at least six of these products are almost identical in composition. The cost, however, differs. This is mainly due to the formulation and delivery methods.

In 1982, growth hormones were made famous when Dirk Pearson and Sandra Schall published their best-selling book, Life Extension. The book extolled the benefits of human growth hormones. The authors wrote of improving their own physiques by the use of these substances. It increased overall body strength and created muscle bulk as well as improving eyesight and sex drive.

Human growth hormones (HGH), became big news in baseball when Jason Grimsley was caught accepting a package of drugs by the US Postal Service. When questioned, Grimsley admitted his use of steroids, HGH and other drugs, and named a number of former and present teammates as users of performance-enhancing drugs, including amphetamines. What was most startling in his confession was that he used *only* HGH, even after Major League Baseball began its testing program in 2004.

On June 6, 2006, agents searched a warehouse in which they believed Grimsley had stored amounts of HGH that he planned to distribute. When questioned, some players said that they took the substances because they had a healing quality that helped them with their injuries. This was far from the truth. In fact, human growth hormones increase the number of red blood cells, boost heart function, and make more energy available by stimulating the breakdown of fat, improving eyesight, providing better sleep and better sex.

With exercise, muscles grow faster and stronger and speed and reflexes are improved. Side effects are considered reasonably mild but can be very serious, especially when the ingredient is taken in excessive amounts or used over prolonged periods. One such side effect is called, acromegaly. It is a disease characteristic of excessive growth in the head, feet and limbs. The lips, nose, tongue, jaws and forehead all increase in size and the fingers and toes widen and become spade- like. The organs of the digestive system may also increase in size, which may cause heart failure. Excessive HGH use in adults may also lead to diabetes.

Another shocking incident occurred around this same time, in 2002, when Ken Caminiti told Sports Illustrated that he was using steroids at various times during his career, including the period during which he was selected as the Most Valuable Player Award in the National League in 1998. He also stated that he believed that 50% of all the players were using performance enhancing drugs.

Caminiti played most of his career for the Houston Astros, but he also played for the San Diego Padres for three years and helped them to reach the World Series in 1995. He finished his career with the Texas Rangers and the Atlanta Braves. The Braves, however, dropped him in 2001. Eight days later, he was arrested for possession of cocaine. He pleaded guilty and was given three years probation. A Houston judge revoked his probation for failing his fourth drug test. He then received 180 days in jail, but was given credit for time served already and was released. Caminiti died on October 10, 2004, from a massive heart attack. He was *only* 41 years old.

It is virtually impossible to give an exact date when the Steroid Era in baseball began. Obviously, many players were long term users before the public became aware that the use of drugs violated the rules of baseball. A reasonable guess would be from 1998 to 2006. The high point of the era occurred when Mark McGuire, Sammy Sosa, and Barry Bonds were hitting balls out of ballparks with great regularity. In June of 1998, Sammy Sosa hit 20 home runs. There is no doubt that these players were all great home run hitters and did not need to be using performance enhancing drugs.

The following is a chart of the home run production of <u>Sosa</u>, <u>Bonds</u>, and <u>McGuire</u> from 1995 to 2005.

Home Run Chart

Year	Sosa	Bonds	McGuire
1995	36	33	
1996	40	42	39
1997	36	40	52
1998	66	37	58
1999	63	34	34
2000	50	49	24
2001	64	73	70
2002	49	46	65
2003	40	45	32
2004	35	45	29
2005	14	5	0

Do these statistics suggest anything to you? Using Barry Bonds as an example, when he was 30 years old, he hit 40 home runs. When he was 35, he hit 73 home runs. One might ask the question, how did he get so good so fast at age 35 when most players are in the twilight phase of their careers? Incidentally, the New York Times reported that in 1993, Sammy Sosa tested positive for performance enhancing substances. He was one of 104 that were reported to have tested positive for substance use.

The Mitchell Report

In March of 2006, Baseball Commissioner Bud Selig, announced that former United States Senator, George Mitchell, would head up an individual investigation into the illegal use of steroids and other performance enhancing substances in Major League Baseball. The players union was largely uncooperative in providing any information to the Mitchell committee. As a matter of fact, a memo was sent out to all players stating that they should not cooperate or give interviews to anyone from the Mitchell committee. Only one player, Frank Thomas, then with the Toronto Blue Jays, was willing to be interviewed.

So how did the Mitchell committee obtain most of the information to complete their report? Kirk Radomski, a former clubhouse employee for the New York Mets was a critical source of information, providing most of the names that were not generally known to the public at that time. Mitchell was able to secure Radomski's cooperation through San Francisco US Attorney General Scott School's office. Radomski had been charged with distribution of a controlled substance and money laundering and faced up to 30 years in prison. He reached a plea bargaining arrangement in exchange for his cooperation with the Mitchell investigation.

After 27 months of investigations, the Mitchell Report was released on December 13, 2007. Eighty-nine players were named in the report as either users, distributors or those associated with the use and distribution of performance enhancing substances. There were 18 recommendations in the report. Baseball Commissioner Bud Selig said that he would implement all 18 recommendations. Bear in mind, the Baseball Commissioner's authority is limited by what can be accomplished through collective bargaining between the players and the owners.

Historically, when the players union was asked to make certain concessions, they always reponded that nothing can be done unless it has been approved by the collective bargaining agreement with baseball's management. One of George Mitchell's recommendations was that none of the players named in the report should have their careers adversely affected. Commissioner Seelig said that he would take that suggestion under consideration and review the reports on a case-by-case basis to make a determination as to what further action should be taken. During this time, Jason Giambi who had been a member of the New York Yankees said, "Baseball should apologize to America".

In 2004, mandatory random drug testing was initiated. At every stage in the testing process, the players union resisted having their players tested. After a public outrage and a warning from the Congress of the United States, which stated, " If you do not beef up your drug testing program, we will initiate legislation and do it for you", the attitude of the players union seemed to change somewhat and they initiated a reasonably effective testing program. There would be regular testing of all players from spring training through the end of the season. There would be random testing year-round. For example, if a player lived in Red Wing, Minnesota, on December 23, the doorbell might ring and a representative from Major League Baseball would ask the player to void a urine specimen for testing purposes. The punishment for positive testing is as follows: the first offense—a 50 game suspension, the second offense—a 100 game suspension, the third offense—a lifetime ban from baseball.

One basic reason baseball had to get the drug problem under control was the affect it would have on the youth of America. For example, after Mark McGuire admitted that he was taking Anodyne, a steroid precursor, the sale of this supplement increased 1000%. The National Institute on Drug Abuse stated that 8% of high school athletes had used this drug. Baseball players and players in all major sports are role models for young athletes. These young people look to the professional athlete for guidance and direction. This is why the steroid problem was so serious.

One simple fact stands out above all others. These three words, "Performance Enhancing Drugs", tells you the reason and the indictment. Those that were users were cheaters. Just think about it. A player had made the big leagues; he was making millions of dollars; he was given a very special opportunity and a God-given talent. But in spite of that, he still had to cheat. This means he cheated the players who were clean. He cheated the fans that believed in him and the kids who emulated him. He cheated America. A dark black stain had been cast over our national pastime. It wasn't only the players who were involved. It was those that were complicit in knowing what was going on: the owners, the union and the players.

And what about this? What do we do with the records? I believe, as does United States Senator, Jim Bunning, Hall of Fame Inductee, that any records compiled by known cheaters should be expunged from the record books.

And what about the Hall of Fame? Why should we honor and enshrine these cheaters and put them in the same high place as we do the greatest players who have ever played the game? This is one reason I have the greatest admiration for Henry Hank Aaron. He broke Babe Ruth's record of total home runs of 714 with a bat and those lightening fast wrists, not with the pill and the needle.

Hopefully this sad chapter in our national pastime is behind us.

CHAPTER

Equipment Changes

The equipment changes in Major League Baseball may be of little or no consequence to the average fan, but they have significantly changed the way today's game is played.

BATTING HELMETS

Throughout the history of baseball, pitchers have always thrown at hitters. It is part of what they do. The fear factor or intimidation factor is ever present when a hitter walks into the batter's box. On August 17, 1920 a player named Ray Chapman was playing for the Cleveland Indians. Their opponent was the New York Yankees. Chapman was struck around his ear by a pitch thrown by the Yankee pitcher Carl May. With help, Ray Chapman staggered to his feet and then collapsed; he never regained consciousness and died the next day. It took baseball 51 years to come to grips with this problem. In 1971, Major League Baseball required that all batters wear a protective batting helmet. Ear flaps were added shortly after that, and ultimately helmets were acquired to be worn when running the bases. In addition to the helmets, baseball directed umpires now to enforce the rules against pitchers throwing at hitters. Prior to 1971, there was no such enforcement; retaliation was meted out by the player or players of the other team.

GLOVES AND MITTS

The size and design of gloves and mitts have also been drastically changed. Many of the great catches we see today called "web gems" would not have happened 50 years ago. Years back, gloves were much smaller and did not have the extensive webbing of the present day gloves and mitts. With the exception of the first baseman, infielders' gloves are larger than the old ones, but smaller than the outfielders' gloves. The reason for the smaller glove is to enable the infielder to transfer the ball from the glove to the hand more quickly to make, for example, a double-play. The outfielder's glove has slightly longer fingers and a loose webbing connecting the individual fingers creating a net like effect so that the outfielder can more easily snag fly balls.

CATCHERS EQUIPMENT

The largest number of changes in equipment since the helmet have been to the catcher's gear. Catcher has always been the most dangerous position on the team and the one that has sustained the greatest number of injuries. The consistency with which catchers were getting beat up behind the plate prompted the saying "the catchers equipment are the tools of ignorance". Much has changed over the last several years to make catching safer. Today, many fans may not realize that catchers do not catch as they once did. The primary reason they don't is due to a change in design of the catcher's mitt. The old-style mitt was fat and round and resembled a small inner tube. It had a pocket in the center to receive the ball. The unprotected throwing arm and hand assisted in catching the ball. This fact alone was the cause of many injuries.

The catcher's mitt has been completely redesigned. Much of the padding has been removed and a large leather web has been installed at the back of the mitt connecting either side by leather thongs. This configuration allows the catcher to open and close the mitt in a hinging action when receiving the ball. The ball is caught in the pocket formed by the large leather webbing.

No longer does the catcher have his hand directly behind the pocket because of this change in design. As a result, all Major League catchers now catch the ball one-handed. Before the pitcher delivers the ball, the catcher tucks his right hand behind his right thigh. That right arm and hand are used for throwing and helping assist when balls are thrown in the dirt (there are no lefthanded catchers in baseball).

Another major change is the redesign of the catchers mask. Many catchers, but not all, wear masks copied from the hockey goalie mask. They are pointed in a more downward direction and give better protection to the neck area. They also have a built in helmet to protect the back of the catchers head. Some batters have a long follow through after they have swung at the ball; the bat comes around and can strike the catcher in the back of his head. With the built-in helmet, this problem is solved.

The catcher's shin guards have also been improved for greater protection and flexibility. An extended flap is attached to the bottom of the shin guard that goes over the catcher's foot. In addition, the chest protector has been improved to include shoulder flaps that partially protect the catcher from foul tips. Prior to this improvement, foul tips would hit the edge of the catcher's shoulder where was no padding. Improvements have also been made in athletic supporters to protect the catcher in the private area. It may be of interest that all infielders and pitchers wear an athletic supporter with a pouch which is installed with a curved metal cup that is held in place with snaps.

BATS

In 1927, when Babe Ruth hit 60 home runs, he used a 36 inch long bat that weighed 42 ounces. By today's standards that was considered a monster. All modern day players use much lighter bats. One might ask the question; doesn't it take a heavy bat to hit the ball a great distance? How can one hit a ball the same distance with a much lighter bat? The answer is that better weight distribution and design makes the bats more efficient.

There are three elements that are necessary to reach the optimum design of the modern day bat, mass, speed and strength. From experience, I would say that in the late 1950s, the average ballplayer used a 34" or 35" long bat that weighed 34 or 34 1/2 ounces. Today, the average player uses a 34" or 34 1/2 " long bat that weighs between 31 and 32 1/2 ounces. How can the three elements mentioned above be blended together to achieve the optimum results? The answer is by changing the shape of the bat and taking out wood that is not needed. All bats are made on a wood lathe.

Remember that the three essential elements, mass, speed and strength must be maintained in the bat's design. So let's start with the mass. The barrel of the bat is the mass to be swung. From a point just above the trademark and below the barrel, the lathe operator begins to shave the wood at a slightly more abrupt angle than in the older designed bats. He continues to shave away more wood making the handle even thinner. When he is finished, the bat appears to have a very large barrel (which it does not) and a very thin handle. Remember, we are only talking about reducing the weight of the bat by about 2 1/2 ounces.

So what have we accomplished? With the same amount of mass, we have a barrel, and a skinny handle that can swing the mass faster and still be strong enough not to break when striking the baseball. The thickness of the bat below the barrel has been made thinner and the handle even thinner. With a very thin handle and the same amount of mass, the bat can be swung faster without the loss of any power.

Yet, the shape of the bat has been changed and now it would appear that the barrel is larger than it was before, which is not the case. Some players even lighten the weight of the bat by taking out some of the wood at the very top of the bat and honing out about a half inch of wood. Though not exactly, the bat now looks more like an Indian club used by jugglers, then did the old-time bats.   The above principle is no different then with the club in golf. When steel shafts were replaced with graphite shafts, the shafts were as strong as steel, but much lighter and could generate greater club head speed. Lighter bats produce faster bat speed.

Historically, Major League bats were all made of a northern white ash. Wood ash forests can be found in northern Pennsylvania bordering New York State and other northern states such as Michigan. Ash trees are slow-growing and are harvested when the tree is about 50 years old. The best 10% of the wood is used to make bats. Hillrich and Bradsby (Louisville Slugger) have been the major manufacturers of baseball bats, since the latter part of the 19th century. This company still commands 60% of the market. Maple bats have made their way into the industry and command a lesser percentage. Northern white ash may become an endangered species, the reason being that an insect called the Emerald Ash Borer, which is native to Asia has been destroying thousands and thousands of northern white ash trees all over the northern part of the United States.

There is a crash program underway to eliminate

this pest; otherwise the entire ash population could be wiped out.

BASEBALLS

Major League Baseballs have an interesting story to tell us. Today in the modern era, I would venture to say that most readers would be surprised to learn that all Major League baseballs are still hand sewn as they have been for the last 100 years. The Rawlings Corporation has had a facility in Costa Rica, near the capital of San Jose since 1986. Over 300 women turn out between two and 2.2 million baseballs per year using two needles and a red wax cotton thread to sew the covers onto baseballs. Another interesting fact about Major League baseballs most fans do not know is that before each game, the home team set aside 90 baseballs which are hand rubbed by the umpires or their staff with a special dirt supplied by Major League Baseball. This is done to take the shine off of the leather.

UNIFORMS

Gone are the days, of the heavy wool baggy pants uniforms. They have been replaced by an attractive, more formfitting uniform that is much more functional. The old cotton/wool material has been replaced by a smooth and harder knit that is much more attractive. Most players prefer to use the long legs that extend to the tops of the shoes. Some players however prefer the old traditional look of the long stockings that are tucked under the pant leg, just below the knee. In the older era there was a set routine for putting on the socks and the pants.

One would need a stool to get the job done. Most players use 2 pair of socks; one is a white sanitary hose that is pulled and goes over the knee. The other sock is heavy wool, which may have stripes or some other markings and also comes up over the knee. The sanitary hose is used so that if the player should get spiked, there would be something new and clean next to the wound. The heavier outside hose has a strap that goes under the instep and has no heal or toe. This is pulled over the sanitary hose. Then the pants are put on and pulled over both socks just below the knee.

The "knickers" type pants have elastic that fits just below the player's knee. In this position, the socks are folded over the elastic of the pant leg and then the pants are pulled up in the normal fashion.. This makes for a neat looking uniform.

Being of the old-school, I prefer this look to the long leg look most players have adopted today. The home team wears white uniform and the visiting team uses some form of gray uniform (Today, in many cases, a colored shirt is worn with the white or gray pants.) I suppose, the home white arrangement was instituted to make the home team look good. Most teams wear caps that fit well with the colors of the uniform. Occasionally on some throwback days, the teams will wear uniforms and caps from an older era.

BATTING GLOVES

The origin of the batting glove is an off shoot of the glove worn by almost all golfers. Some say Bobby

Thompson was the first to experiment with these gloves in 1949. Ken "Hawk" Harrelson first wore the glove after a round of golf. Rusty Staub was the first player to use gloves on a regular basis. By the early 1980's, batting gloves became an essential part of a player's equipment and a huge new industry was born.

Players wear these gloves because they say it gives them a superior grip. Spitting in your hand with a little bit of dirt is over, for from the big leagues to the little leagues, everyone is wearing batting gloves. Another reason the gloves are worn is that they give the hitter a small amount of protection when struck in the wrist or upper hand by a thrown ball and they ease the sting somewhat when the ball is struck near the handle of the bat. The gloves fit snugly and are held in place with strong velcro strips. Some players hold the gloves in their hands when running the bases; apparently the gloves protect their hands from injury while sliding into bases.

CHAPTER

Pitching Changes and Hitting

Before we get into the pitching changes that have occurred since 1947, I want to give the reader an idea of how difficult it is to hit a 90 mile an hour fastball. The pitching rubber is 60' 6" from home plate. Is that really the true distance that the ball travels from the pitcher to the plate? Let's assume that a pitcher is 6' 4" tall and has a stride of 5 feet. When he takes his windup, makes his stride to home plate, and releases the ball, the distance *is not* 60' 6" but *is* more accurately *about* 55 feet. It takes a baseball traveling at 90 miles an hour .458 seconds to reach home plate. So what does this really mean? Simply stated, the batter has less than half a second to make up his mind and make all of the physical adjustments necessary to hit the baseball. Some of the decisions he must make are: is the ball high or low, inside or outside; what type of pitch is that - is it a fastball, curveball, slider or some other variation? I think that we can agree that hitting a swiftly moving ball is not an easy task.

Ted Williams humorously replied to a writer when asked what was the most difficult thing to do in any sport, "Hitting a baseball consistently." In the group, there was another ballplayer who at that time had a batting average of .220. This player said, " Why are you asking *him* how hard it is, why don't you ask me?" Ted Williams was considered by many to be **the** greatest hitter of all times in the major leagues. In 1941, the season was coming to a close in the American League and the Philadelphia Athletics played the Boston Red Sox in a double header at Fenway Park on the last day. Williams was hitting .401 before the start of the first game and the Boston manager, Joe Cronin, told Williams it would be all right if he wanted to sit out the two games and preserve his .401 average. Williams said he would not have earned his average if he didn't play in the last two games.

The manager of the Philadelphia Athletics was legendary Connie Mack (Cornelius McGillicuddy). McGillicuddy always managed from the dugout in a suit and tie and wore a straw hat. Everyone called him Mr. Mac. When Williams came up to bat for the first time, the catcher told him that Mr. Mac said they were going to pitch to him as in a regular game – no funny stuff, like walking him every time he got up to the plate. Williams came up to bat eight times in the two games. He got 6 hits in 8 times at bat and didn't hit .401 but ended the season at .406.

Ted fought in the Korean War as a fighter pilot and had many close calls. Together with his service in World War II, he lost almost five years from his time as a baseball player. Those years, between ages

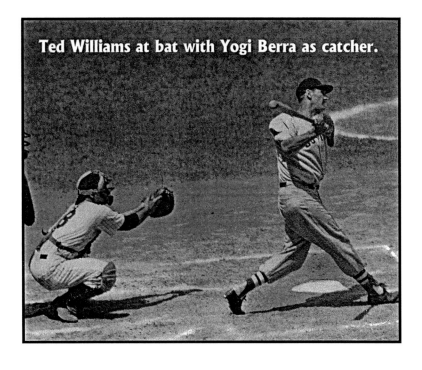

Ted Williams at bat with Yogi Berra as catcher.

27-32 are usually the most productive in a ballplayers career. The year after getting out of the armed services, Ted Williams hit .380. After a 21 year career in baseball, he retired in 1960, but during his last game and last at bat, Ted Williams hit a home run.

I am firmly convinced, that it is more difficult to hit a baseball today than it was in the earlier era. This can also be borne out by a drop in the average of batting averages. Just imagine this unbelievable fact. In 1929, Lefty Grove won twenty-eight games and lost five. In 1930, he won thirty games and lost four. That's fifty-eight won and nine lost. One Sports writer, Arthur "Bugs" Baer, wrote that Lefty could throw a lamb chop past a wolf.

Prior to 1947, and especially in Lefty Grove's day, when a manager handed the ball to his starting pitcher, he expected him to pitch nine innings. In the exceptional case when he could not finish the game, another pitcher was called in from the bullpen to finish. There were no pitch counts at that time and no specialty relief pitchers.

There is an interesting story told about Jim Palmer when he pitched for the Baltimore Orioles in 1970. He was sitting next to his manager Earl Weaver and was charting pitches, which was done if he would be the starting pitcher the next day. He said to his manager "Skip, our pitcher has already thrown 133 pitches." His manager said to him "Take your notepad and your pencil and go and sit at the end of the bench. I'll tell you when our guy is tired!" So much for pitch counts.

Today, if a starting pitcher has six good innings, he is presumed to have had a successful game. True relief pitchers, began to appear in the late '40s and early '50s. Jim Konstanty of the Philadelphia Phillies was the first well-known relief pitcher (1944–1956). Clem Labine (1950–1960) and Johnny Kleppstein (1950-1967) were two more well recognized relief pitchers.

Pitching philosophy was materially changed by the use of early pitching specialists. In today's game, two types of pitchers have developed: starting pitchers and relief pitchers. The relief pitcher category can be broken down further as a short reliever, a long reliever, a setup man and a closer or any variety thereof. Today a relief pitcher may be called in to pitch to one or two batters; another may be called in to pitch to a left- or right-handed batter, depending on the situation. There have been games in which six relief pitchers have appeared in one inning. The main idea here is to put the pitcher in with the best percentage chance of getting the hitter out. The batters job is made more difficult because he is always facing a fresh pitcher trained to get him out.

Another major change today is the different types of pitches that have been developed. In the earlier era, pitchers had three basic pitches; a fastball, a curveball and a change of pace. There were a few pitchers that had a specialty pitch such as a knuckleball or a screwball.

Some pitchers developed a sharp breaking curveball or downer as it was sometimes called. As it approached the hitting area, it would break down sharply. Some ballplayers referred to a good curveball as exploding or falling off the table when it reached the hitting area. One of the most famous pitchers who had developed a specialty pitch, was Hoyt Wilhelm, who, having not only developed it, also pitched the knuckleball until he reached the age of 50. The knuckleball is gripped by the knuckles or by the fingernails dug into the baseball stitching. It is released with no wrist action, and it does not spin; it sails. As it reaches the home plate area, it dives, cuts or breaks in an unusual manner. Even the pitcher does not know what the ball is going to do.

The following is a true story about Hoyt Wilhelm's knuckleball. He had a catcher whose name was Gus Treondous. It was almost comical to watch him try to catch the fluttering ball. Gus had a huge catcher's mitt; it was three times the size of the normal mitt. He couldn't actually catch the ball, so he would slap at it and knock it down and then pick it up. It was equally funny to watch the best hitters in the world try to hit Wilhelm's dancing dervish of a baseball. One said it was like trying to eat Jell-O with boxing gloves on. Another said that hitters looked like they were killing snakes at the plate.

Wilhelm's catcher had more passed balls than any other catcher. A passed ball is a pitched ball that in the opinion of the official scorer should be caught. If the ball is not caught and a runner advances, the catcher is charged with an error. The wild pitch, on the other hand, is a pitched ball that the catcher cannot catch and if a runner advances, the pitcher is charged with the error. Because no catcher could handle him, Wilhelm was traded in 1958 to Baltimore. He had a long and successful career and in 1986, he was inducted into the Baseball Hall of Fame. He was a much traveled player and played with nine Major League teams, compiling a lifetime record of 142 wins, 122 losses. He was the first pitcher to have 200 saves and the first to appear in 1,000 games.

In the modern era, pitchers have developed a variety of new pitches and have learned that by applying pressure of their fingers while gripping the ball, they can affect certain changes in the balls action. The three major pitches that have been developed are the slider, the split finger fastball and the cut fastball or cutter. The slider has a side and downward trajectory breaking into a left-handed hitter, or away from a right-handed hitter, assuming that the pitcher is right-handed. The pitch is very effective in getting hitters out because from a hitter's perspective, as the ball approaches the plate, it looks like a fastball and then slides away and down.

The split finger fastball was developed by Roger Craig, a Major League pitcher and later the manager of the San Francisco Giants from 1986 to 1990. With this particular pitch, the ball is held by the space between the first two fingers of the throwing hand. One must have long fingers and a hand big enough to accommodate the ball. Many pitchers who are not pitching are seen sitting on the bench stretching their fingers with the baseball. The ball has a tumbling action, and as with the slider, looks like a fastball and then breaks down sharply.

The cut fastball or cutter is a pitch that has been made famous by the New York Yankees great closer, Mariano Rivera. By adjusting the middle finger on the ball and by twisting the wrist at the release point, the ball moves laterally in or away from the hitter, making it difficult to be hit squarely on the bat. It moves 4 to 5 inches, but that is enough to disrupt the hitter's timing. Hitters in the older era did not have to face these three pitches. This is another way that pitchers are ganging up on hitters.

All pitchers today and in the past throw some type of change of pace pitch. The main object is to deceive the hitter by the same motion, and arm angle making him think that the pitcher is throwing a fastball when, in actuality, the change of pace comes in somewhat slower and again disrupts the hitter's timing.

I have often been asked the question, "Do pitchers today throw harder than pitchers did before 1947?" The answer is "Yes". There were *many* who threw that hard, but today *almost all* pitchers throw 90 miles an hour. No one can deny that there were pitchers like Bob Feller, "Bullet" Bob Turley, or "Goose" Gossage and many others who threw as hard as present-day pitchers, but today there are just *many more* of them. Bear in mind, that in that era, there were only sixteen teams. Now there are thirty. I asked a Major League scout, what he looked for in a pitching prospect. He replied, "If they don't throw 90 miles an hour, we don't look at them".

The biggest change in pitching in the modern era that transcends all others is the introduction of relief pitching. Complete games by a starting pitcher are going to be a thing of the past and unfortunately, I believe that the era of the 300 game winning pitcher or even a 250 game, for that matter, is over. The different pitches that are thrown today may have been a natural evolution, but the introduction of the relief pitching has materially changed the game from what it was. Today, very few pitchers ever pitch the full nine innings.

CHAPTER  10

Fitness and Conditioning

In the older era, we were told that too much swimming or weightlifting would develop the wrong kinds of muscles and would make us muscle bound. This concept proved to be completely false. Most baseball thinking at that time was that players played themselves into shape and didn't need any other conditioning exercise. It would be hard for us to envision Ted Williams or Joe DiMaggio toiling in the weight room doing heavy bench presses or squats to improve their performance skills. One might ask the question, why was there not more emphasis placed on players conditioning? The answer is because medical science had not yet fully determined how much and what kinds of exercises are beneficial to the general public and to professional athletes in particular. As medical knowledge increased, so did the implementation and use of conditioning programs to improve the skills of these gifted athletes.

I am sure that most of us do not give a lot of thought to how difficult it is to become a professional athlete. For example, in America there are about 2 million boys at all stages from Little League baseball to American Legion baseball to industrial baseball to semi-pro baseball to all the other venues where young people play baseball. Add to this a total of 10 million adults throughout the world who also play baseball. Now if we take the 30 teams that play and we multiply them by 30 players per team, we will get a total of 900 players. Nine hundred players out of a total of 10 or 12 million is a pretty rarefied area to be in. Fans sometimes asked the question, "How can a team keep the player who has a batting average of only 215?" The answer is, there is *no one* who could be found who could do any *better*. With the extensive scouting systems that Major League Baseball has today, no one from the eighth grade on is overlooked; they don't miss anybody.

Training and conditioning

These are two very different concepts. For example, let's take a heavyweight boxer who is going into training for a championship fight. He may set up a camp in some remote area for a period of three or more months. The idea here is to get him into peak condition for the big fight. Everything he does is focused on that objective. He may go on a specialized nutritional diet; do a lot of roadwork, such as running; engage in a great deal of weight training; spar with several sparring partners; practice hitting the light and heavy bag along with many other activities that fighters concentrate on when preparing for a big fight. Most of us are also familiar with the intense training that is required by the many dedicated athletes before the Olympic Games.

The concept of conditioning for a Major League Baseball player is vastly different. It is a process of adding to what the player is already doing, knowing that the long grind of a 162 game season lies ahead. Bear in mind, that before each game, players take batting practice, infield practice and a series of stretching exercises.

Slowly but surely weightlifting has become a major part of the conditioning philosophy. I would venture to say, that there is not a team in the major or minor leagues, which does not have a fully equipped weight training facility. Players are required to participate on a regular schedule as prescribed by the strength coach and other trainers. Stretching of the muscles is important to all of us, especially athletes who stretch their muscles to the maximum. Proper stretching can guard against hamstring tears and torn groin muscles which are very difficult and slow to heal.

Spring training, then and now.

Money has always played an important role in decisions; remember rule one? So what has this got to do with spring training? Simply this - in 1947, the average salary for a big-league baseball player was $11,000 a year. Obviously the best player made more money than that, but that was the average. Because of the low salaries, most players had to find work in the off-season to pay the bills and provide for their families.

Many at that time, were not well educated and had to find work in factories or other similar employment. This left little time or desire to engage in any kind of a meaningful conditioning program. There were no rules or guidelines for diet or nutrition. Most, but not all, drank beer and usually gained weight in the off-season. As a result, they came to his spring training out of shape. The main purpose of spring training, at that time, was to get back into playing shape.

Thus, the players would head for the sunny climes of Florida to sweat and to strain themselves back into proper playing condition. Running, calisthenics, stretching drills and eventually inter-squad games were what the doctor ordered, so to speak. Some that really needed to lose weight would wear a rubberized sweatshirt that would cause the player to sweat profusely. This thinking didn't seem to work out very well, because as soon as the player drank an abundant amount of water, he would gain the weight right back.

Today's players are valuable commodities and as a result, the teams keep a very close eye on their million-dollar babies. Most teams have a year round conditioning program. As a result, most players come to spring training in shape, not playing shape, but physical shape... As a result, within a week of the start of spring training, teams begin playing a schedule of spring training games. Usually spring training starts about March 1st each year; the teams play about 28 games before breaking camp and head to their respective cities to start the regular season, which usually occurs about April 5 of each year.

In this chapter, we have discussed the early period which did not emphasize the need for regular physical conditioning. Then we looked at the most recent. A period in which great emphasis has been placed on conditioning, nutrition, and the overall physical condition of Major League Baseball players.

Now we are entering into a new and exciting period that I will call the *speed and motion period.* If you recall, in Chapter 8, Equipment Changes, we discussed at length the successful efforts of increasing the bat speed by reducing the overall weight and changing the shape of modern-day bats. The new conditioning thinking, takes this concept of speed and movement to a new dimension. It reduces the need for heavy weight lifting.

In this new system, players use only their own weight and body movement to build strength and agility. There is no question that being strong is an essential part and important attribute to any major league baseball player. Weight training, certainly increases muscle mass and makes one stronger, but does it make a player appreciably faster and quicker? Strengthening of the core muscles is another key to this new system and if successful, this system may replace at least in part, the need for any heavy weight training.

Professional dancers, yoga and Pilates practitioners develop strong core muscles from their training. What are the core muscles? They are the unseen heroes of our lower abdominal and lower back muscles. They are the muscles that hold our hip girdle secure. They are unseen, because they are under the more visible muscles. For example, the transverse abdominal is hidden under our rectus abdominis, our visible abs, if you have visible abs. The core muscles work in helping you to have a good posture and they protect many of our internal organs. Strong core muscles are essential for lower back health and will add to your power moves, especially if you are an athlete. If one can maintain strong core muscles, your body can benefit long into old age.

Baseball and martial arts principles.

I have long believed that if baseball could adapt the principles of those who are proficient in the martial arts such as judo, jujitsu and Taekwondo, they could employ the principles of speed and movement to the built-in athleticism of modern-day ballplayers and their skills could be greatly enhanced. As a result of playing and managing in the minor leagues, I have learned that all great hitters hit with their hips. Two good examples of this fact are Ted Williams and Paul Moliter. They both had two things in common; they waited for the absolute last instant to swing the bat and when they did swing, their hips exploded.

We may be approaching a new era in how

baseball players and other athletes are conditioned. The Seattle Mariners are the first Major League team to implement this new system. I am very optimistic and hope that the new concept will be successful. The information regarding this new conditioning program to be implemented by the Seattle Mariners came from an article appearing in the Seattle Times by Geoff Baker. The new program was developed by Dr. Marcus Elliott and is called Peak Performance Project: P3. Dr. Elliott will be the Mariners new director of sports science and performance.

CHAPTER

The Designated Hitter Rule

From the inception of the game until 1973, baseball was always played with nine players on offense and nine players on defense. The pitcher would take his turn when it came up in the batting order and went back on the field as would any other defensive player after the inning was over.

On January 11, 1973, the owners of 24 Major League teams voted to allow teams in the American League to use the designated hitter rule. This enabled another player to bat for the pitcher while still allowing the pitcher to stay in the game. The idea of adding a 10th man to the baseball lineup was not new and had been suggested by Connie Mack as far back as 1928 and also in 1970 by Charlie Finley of the Oakland Athletics. They suggested that a good hitter replace the pitcher who generally was not a good hitter when his turn came up in the lineup. They believed this would add extra offensive punch to the lineup and would draw more fans to the ball parks.

Bear in mind that in the 70's the country was in a minor recession. There were oil shortages and cars were standing in long gas lines for hours. Obviously attendance in ball parks, especially in the American League dropped. Adding the designated hitter rule would increase attendance. It all goes back to Rule One, which is *"It all boils down to the money"*.

Their reasoning was that this would help the American League which lagged behind the National League in both scoring and attendance. The National League resisted this change for itself and for the first time in baseball history, the two leagues would be playing under different rules. This marked the biggest rule change in Major League Baseball since 1903 when it was decided that foul balls would be counted as strikes. Although the designated hitter rule initially began as a three-year experiment, it would be permanently adopted by all American League teams and later by most amateur and most minor league teams.

The designated hitter rule essentially split Major League Baseball into two separate and distinct games; changing how they had been played and managed for the last 100 years. Instead of nine players playing against nine players in the American League, we now have 10 players playing against ten players. The role of the pitcher as a member of the lineup has been completely changed because he never comes to bat. When his turn in the lineup comes up, a designated hitter is inserted into the lineup and takes the pitchers turn at bat. When the inning is over the designated hitter sits down in the dugout and chews bubblegum and the pitcher takes his place on the mound. I guess the days of Red Man, Beachnut and Mail Pouch chewing tobacco are gone forever.

From the beginning, baseball purists argued that the designated hitter rule took away from baseball the integrity that it had enjoyed from the onset. The rift between pro-and anti-designated hitter fans has continued to the present day. At first, the designated hitter rule did not apply to any game in the World Series in which American League and National League winners met for the world championship. From 1976 to 1985 it applied only to the series held in even numbered years and in 1986 the current rule took effect, according to which the designated hitter rule is used or not used depending on the practice of the home team.

It would be similar to having the National Football League use Canadian football rules for one half of the Super Bowl game.

Most of us are familiar with the story and the movie, *The Fiddler on the Roof.* The lead actor, the father, Tevye, told his daughter who was considering marrying a man not of the Jewish faith that she could not do it because of tradition. It is similar to a bird being in love with a fish. That would be nice but where would they live? There are so many arguments for and against the designated hitter rule that we will try to examine the more glaring of these and how it has changed our national pastime.

One area where the designated hitter rule may not be apparent to the average fan, but is significant to those who play the game, is in the American League where the pitcher never comes to bat. As previously noted, pitchers have historically thrown at hitters; it's happened since the inception of the game. When the pitcher came to bat, the other pitcher could retaliate by throwing at him. With the designated hitter rule, the pitcher never bats and the other team can never really retaliate. It may seem like a small thing, but it is not so small when you're making your living playing baseball and need to protect yourself.

This designated hitter rule also makes it more difficult to manage in one of the Leagues. In the National League, strategies such as double switches; changes in the lineup to accommodate pitchers positioned for bunting; and other adjustments must be decided upon. In the American League, all the manager is asked to do is to manage nine hitters and concentrate his main efforts on the starting pitchers and relief pitchers. It is not so easy in the National League.

It has been said that one of the reasons for the designated hitter rule is to prolong the playing years of a good hitter who no longer has the agility or the leg speed to be a position player. He can prolong his career for as many as five or six years as a designated hitter. The National League does not enjoy this luxury. The leagues are not equal. These differences may never be resolved and if it is left to the unions and collective bargaining, the unions may be reluctant to want to see these highly paid designated hitters' positions abolished.

In addition to the discussion above we haven't even touched on the problems that the designated hitter rule has on inter league play, the All-Star game and the World Series, all of which are affected in some degree by the designated hitter rule. Traditionalists would prefer to see the game go back to nine players who are playing against nine players and the pitcher taking his turn at bat as they always did. However, it has become a money game and most decisions, if not all, are determined by their impact on the bottom line.

Another unforeseen consequence that occurred when they began the designated hitter rule resulted from the fact that they did not anticipate all of the ramifications of this rule when interleague games began in 1997. The interleague games create something of a dilemma when using the designated hitter rule as some pitchers in the American League playing in National League parks have never batted. As a matter of fact, most of them don't even take batting practice with their regular lineups on their own teams because it is unnecessary.

When they are playing in a National League the pitchers are required to bat and some are really lost when they get into the batter's box. In 2010, when Mariano Rivera of the Yankees had to bat in an interleague game it was amusing to see how awkward he was because he had never batted in a regular game before. To his credit, he did make contact and hit a ground ball. It is also important to note here that when the lineup cards are prepared and presented to the umpire, the designated hitter's name and place in the batting order must be present.

The future is never certain, therefore, no one can tell if we will ever see the day where we have our national pastime essentially playing the same game again.The designated hitter rule will either be abolished or it will some day become uniform in both leagues.

CHAPTER

Umpires

In a book about baseball, it would not seem fitting if there were not a chapter devoted to one of the most important elements of our national pastime - Umpires. Baseball is a game played by three elements: players, managers and umpires. Most fans and most people in America are familiar with names like Babe Ruth, Lou Gehrig, Joe DiMaggio, Ted Williams, Bob Feller, Nolan Ryan and many other great players of the past and present. We also know a great deal about the managers from Connie Mack to Casey Stengel and Bobby Cox. These men have become household names. Yet the third leg of the three-legged stool that makes baseball, the umpires, is virtually unknown to the American people.

The first time we are introduced to them is when we go to the ball park or are watching a game on television. Four men dressed in blue emerge onto the field from their dressing rooms and take a slow but deliberate walk to home plate to meet with the two managers or their representatives to exchange lineup cards and go over the ground rules. We know that about ten minutes after this meeting, the game is going to start. The umpires then take their respective positions, one behind home plate, one at first base, one at second base and one at third.

The remainder of this chapter will be devoted to removing the veil and introducing the reader into the real world of who umpires are, what they must do to become Major League umpires, who they work for, how much money they make, do they have a union and a variety of other facts to help us understand the life of a major league umpire. We will look at the history of umpires, their duties and the honors that have been awarded to the most famous umpires of our national pastime.

A baseball umpire plays an important role in the outcome of any game. The pressure is always on the umpire to be right. Earning a living as an umpire in Major League Baseball or in the minor leagues that supply umpires to the major league teams takes a great deal of training and hard work.

Just like Major League players, umpires must work their way through the ranks of the minor leagues to get the experience and training necessary to make it to the big leagues. According to the MLB Director of the Umpires Association, it usually takes seven to ten years in the minor leagues before an umpire gets to the majors. That is twice the amount of time it takes a good baseball player to get to the big leagues. Another reason it takes so long is because most MLB umps have a long time career with little turnover.

What are the necessary steps that an individual must take if he is serious about becoming a Major League umpire?

1. <u>Enroll</u> in a professional umpire school: There are two training schools in Florida, the Jim Evans Academy of Professional Umpiring operates in Kissimmee, Florida near Disney World and the Harry Wendelstedt School for umpires located in Ormond Beach, which is just north of Daytona Beach, Florida. These are the only two umpire schools approved by the Professional Baseball Umpire Corporation (PBUC) which oversees all professional baseball umpires.

These schools are conducted in the off season of baseball and are five weeks in duration. The combined enrollment in these schools is about 300 students per year. Most of these students have never umpired a game before they go to Umpire School so they must be taught the whole realm of information necessary to be an umpire. The courses are very intense and cover the entire gamut of physical training, rules sessions, hand signals positioning, and every aspect of how to be an umpire on and off the field.

2. <u>Get Noticed</u>: Instructors look for many characteristics other than knowledge of baseball rules when evaluating baseball umpire students. Important traits they are

looking for are confidence, a strong presence on the field, knowledge of mechanics of where to go when the ball is hit, forceful calls, the use of good voice, hustle and ability to handle situations on the field.

Good judgment, common sense and character are three important factors that the trainers evaluate. While knowledge of the rules and mechanics are important, character and integrity are carefully observed by the trainers. Good judgment and character are just as important as the physical attributes of learning to be an umpire. These qualities are not easily learned and when one considers that the integrity of the game is being put into the hands of these young men, these are significant qualities.

   3. Finish at the top of your class: It is of equal importance to be competitive within your class as it is to learning the fundamentals. A student should strive diligently to finish the course in the top 10% of those enrolled. After attending the five-week course during January and prior to February, the top students are selected to attend an evaluation course. It varies each year depending on what openings will be available. Generally 50 students are selected - about 25 from each school.

   4. Being signed to a lower league: At the evaluation course, the instructors monitor the students and make recommendations to the Rookie and Short-Season Class-A League

presidents about possible candidates for hire. Then the new umpires begin their long trek to become Major League umpires. They start off in the minor leagues. The PBUC evaluates the umpires to promote them from one minor-league level to the next until they have reached the AAA level.

At that point, Major League Baseball starts looking at each umpire to decide who is going to come up to the big leagues. This is a long and arduous journey but if one is willing to put in the time and effort, the rewards of being a Major League umpire are well worth it.

Questions and Discussions about Major League Umpires

Who hires major league umpires? Until a few years ago major league umpires were employed and paid by their respective American and National League divisions. Today all umpires work for Major League baseball and are paid salary and expenses pursuant to a collective bargaining agreement the umpires' unions have agreed to. The World Umpire Association union was established in 1969.

How many umpires are on the Major League roster? There are 17 crews of four umpires each or 68 umpires with 22 umpires on option. The umpires rotate positions after each game. One umpire, not necessarily the one behind the plate is appointed as crew chief. He is the one to whom the major decisions are brought.

What is the annual salary of an umpire? The starting salary for a new umpire is approximately $120,000 a year plus expenses; a senior umpire can make as much as $300,000 per year plus expenses.

An interesting fact to note is that under no circumstances are umpires permitted to stay in the same hotels as the ballplayers.

It might be of interest to the reader that when one begins to play professional baseball, he is told that you must never bump, push, or strike an umpire. The penalty for doing any of the above, depending on the severity of the act, could result in lifelong suspension from baseball.

Most baseball players, major or minor, expect the umpires to do two things. First, they expect the umpire to be as consistent as possible and second, they expect the umpire to position himself to make the correct call.

Are umpires graded on a regular basis? Yes, umpires are graded regularly; it is not a point system like being given a 70%, 80% or 90%. It is more or less a pass or fail arrangement. Are umpires evaluated after every game? The answer is yes, they are graded on performance, positioning, enthusiasm decisiveness and a variety of other criteria. Umpires, being human, make errors in judgment; this is only natural. It is similar to a baseball player striking out four times in one ball game and getting three hits and a walk off home run in the next game. Bill Clem, who is regarded as the Dean of all umpires made the statement "I never missed one— in my heart."

EQUIPMENT changes and how they affect the way balls and strikes are now called.

Prior to 1969 all umpires working behind the plate wore a large balloon-like chest protector. With the large cumbersome protector, the umpire worked over the catcher. This gave him a better view of both sides of the plate which is only seventeen inches wide. The large protector somewhat diminished his view of low pitches. Starting in 1969, all umpires were required to use an inside protector that was worn under the uniform. With the change to the inside protector umpires now position themselves almost between the batter and the catcher in the space that exists there.. The umpire now positions himself in that slot and squats down and makes his calls, nearly between the batter and the catcher.

Some say that it limits his view of the outside part of the plate away from the batter. However, the inside protector gives the umpire more flexibility to move his arms and move around the plate area and does not inhibit his movement as it did with the large inflatable protectors.

The inside protector also has built-in shoulder pads that protect the umpire from foul balls. Using the inside protector allows the umpire to call balls and strikes more efficiently and gives him greater flexibility, especially in cases where he must make calls when runners are sliding into home plate and on certain occasions having to run down to third base to cover third-base when that area is vacated by the third-base umpire to go down the left-field line to call a play there. This has been the most dramatic change in umpire equipment that has taken place in the last one hundred years.

The umpires do have the benefit of newly designed shoes that protect their feet especially their toes because they have steel on steel plate just above the bottom of the shoe. In addition their masks have been modified to give them better protection around the neck area with a heavy leather strap that hangs down from the front of the mask.

All in all the new changes have cut down considerably on the injuries that umpires have sustained in the past, however they can't be protected from everything so some foul balls will get through and strike the umpire on the arms, the thighs, the hands, and other places that are difficult to cover. They do of course wear shin guards under their trousers similar to those worn by the catchers.

Working behind the plate is not an easy task when one considers the variety of activities they must perform. For example, during the course of a nine inning game they have to make decisions regarding 200 to 275 pitches. They have to make decisions on whether or not a batter is struck with a thrown ball, and in addition they have to make calls when runners are sliding into home plate. Just consider the fact that a nine inning game may take three hours and the umpires have to stand behind the plate during the entire game. They do not have the luxury of sitting down between innings as the players do. They may go to the dugout for a glass of water or to relieve themselves but other than that they must stand out in the hot sun for three to three and half hours.

The crew that is working the game rotates each game rotating in a clockwise fashion from first base to behind the plate, from the plate to third base, and third base to second base. Each member of the crew has to be proficient in making calls at each of these locations. The umpire at first base knows that in the next game he will be behind the plate and each position requires different movements and hand signals.

Few people are familiar with the technique umpires use to determine safe or out calls at first base. Watching the runner's foot touch first base and watching the ball cannot be done at the same time. To resolve this, the ump watches the foot of the runner as he reaches first base and then listens for the slap in the glove of the first baseman. He then determines which gets there first. This skill is not easy to master, however, when repeated many times during the game, it becomes automatic for the ump to make the right call.

Hall Of Fame Umpires

There are nine umpires that have been inducted into the National Baseball Hall of Fame in Cooperstown, New York, starting in 1953. These umpires, selected by the Veterans Committee were chosen for their outstanding contribution to their profession. The Veterans Committee is part of the framework of the National Baseball Hall of Fame. This committee's responsibility is to choose people who have contributed to the game of baseball other than contemporary players. They make recommendations for inductions on managers, umpires, executives, long time retired players and others who have furthered the game of baseball.

Below is a list of these outstanding umpires and their contribution to baseball.

Inducted in 1953, Tom Connolly – Born Dec. 31, 1870 - Died April 29, 1961.

He became umpire and chief in 1931. He was the first umpire to be elected to the Baseball Hall of Fame. He was born in Manchester, England. Mr. Connolly was associated with the American League for 60 years. He was 90 years old when he died.

Inducted in 1953, Bill Klem – Born February 22, 1874 - Died September 16, 1951.
He is considered to be the father of baseball umpires. He umpired for 37 years, called 5,374 games and retired at age 68. He is probably the most quoted of all umpires. Mr. Klem was widely respected for bringing dignity and professionalism to umpiring.

Inducted in 1973, Billy Evans – Born February 10, 1894 - Died January 23, 1955.

He was known as "The Boy Umpire" because he broke into the Major Leagues at age 22. He was known for his fairness and good judgment. He worked six World Series and enjoyed a 22 year career.

Induced in 1974, Jocko Conlan – Born December 6, 1899 - Died April 16, 1989.

Born in Chicago, Illinois, he began his career as a center fielder in 1934. In 1936 he had an unusual opportunity. During a game against the St Louis Browns, an umpire named Red Ormsby fell ill to heat exhaustion. Conlan was asked to fill in and took to it well. The next year, he made the transition to umpire in the Major Leagues. He umpired from 1941 to 1965, and was in five World Series and six All Star Games.

Inducted in 1976, Cal Hubbard – Born October 31, 1900 - Died October 17, 1976.

Cal Hubbard was a very interesting person. He had a successful football career before he started umpiring. He was elected into the College Football Hall of Fame in 1962. A year later, he was inducted into the National Football Hall of Fame. After football, he turned to baseball as a Major League Umpire. He umpired from 1946 to 1951. His career was cut short by a hunting accident. He was a huge man, 6 feet 4 inches tall, weighing 250 pounds but possessed a gentle spirit. He was a very good umpire.

Inducted in 1989, Al Barlick – Born April 2, 1915 - Died December 27, 1995.

Al Barlick earned the respect of his peers and players with his booming calls and decisive hand signals. Knowledge of the rules, proficiency on balls and strikes, unwavering hustle and a knack of anticipating and defusing rough situations earned him induction into the Baseball Hall of Fame. He had served 33 years as a Major League Umpire, worked seven All Star games and seven World Series. It is considered that the best umpires worked these high profile games. For 22 years after he retired, he worked as a consultant for the major leagues.

Inducted in 1992, Bill McGowan – Born January 18, 1896 - Died December 9, 1954.

He served as an umpire from 1925 to 1954. He was Dean of Umpires. He umpired the last game of the Boston Red Sox 1941 season. In this game, Ted Williams was hitting 401. As Williams stepped into the batters box, Bill McGowan bent down and brushed off home plate. Without raising his head, he said to Ted Williams, "If you are going to hit .400, you have to stay loose." Williams got six hits in eight times at bat and batted .406. No one has matched this record in the succeeding 70 years.

Inducted in 1999, Nestor Chylak – Born May 11, 1922 - Died February 17, 1982.

He was an American League umpire in the post World War II era. He earned the respect of managers and players alike. He served for 25 years. He participated in 3,857 games.

<u>Inducted in 2010, Doug Harvey</u> – Born March 13, 1930 - Still living.

He served from 1962 to 1992 and participated in 4,673 games and was crew chief in the 1964 and 1988 All Star games. He was in five World Series and he umpired in seven All Star games. The American Baseball Research Organization ranked Harvey as the second greatest umpire in history behind Bill Klem.

CHAPTER  13

All Star Game:
Mid Summer Classic

How did it all begin? In the mid-20's Chicago had considered having a world's fair in the early 1930's. It was to be called the Century of Progress Exposition. The theme was exploration, astronomy, electronic development and many other technological breakthroughs that would happen in the next 100 years. Planning for this event started in 1928, where plans were made, contracts were let and the work of planning was in high gear. In all of their planning, the people involved and no one else in the United States knew that on Thursday, October 24, 1929 the stock market would crash and it would be the beginning of an eleven year depression; the worst depression the nation has ever known.

In the planning stages of the World's Fair, the sports editor of the Chicago Tribune, Arch Ward, conceived the idea that in conjunction with the World's Fair, baseball could bring together the greatest players in the American League with the greatest players of the National League and have an All-Star Game showcasing these great players. His vision was that the game would add greatly to the

world's fair and draw more people from all over the
United States especially from the west for this two-
year long world exposition. He convinced the sixteen
owners of the Major League Baseball teams and the
Commissioner of baseball that this would be a
worthy event but would only showcase for one year.

Before going into further detail about the game
itself, it is necessary to understand the times the
country was living in during this period of history.
This book is being written in 2011 when the economy
is in a bad state. But this is nothing to compare
with the Great Depression. For example 25% of the
workforce in the 48 states was out of work and could
not find a job. In this eleven year period, 9000 banks
closed and with the closure of these banks went the
depositors' money that was in those banks.

At that time, there was no Federal Deposit
Insurance Corporation to protect the depositors.
People lost all their money. There were bread lines
in the big cities, where men stood in lines for blocks
in the freezing cold and unbearable heat to get a
bowl of soup and a quarter loaf of bread because
there was nothing to eat. But through it all, the one
thing that people clung to for hope, where there was
no hope, was professional baseball, and the All-Star
game added to that hope.

The first game was held on July 6, 1933 in
Comiskey Park on Chicago's South side. When one
entered Comiskey Park, he had the feeling that he
was in the Roman Coliseum because it was so huge.
The dimensions of the ballpark were enormous, 368

feet down the left and right field line and 445 feet in center field. They also had double deck pavilions in the left and right field that towered four stories above the field.

Some of the greatest players of all time played in the All-Star games starting in 1933. As a matter of fact, seventeen of the eighteen players that started in the 1934 All Star Game are all in the Baseball Hall of Fame. The players were eager to be selected to play in the All-Star game. They wanted to win for their league. Although the game was originally planned to be a one-time event, it was so popular that it became an annual affair and was always played on or about the second Tuesday in July, at various ballparks around the country.

In the 1934 All-Star game there occurred one of the greatest pitching performances of all time. Carl Hubbell was pitching for the National League and in the first inning Charlie Garringer reached first base on a single, then there was a walk, and coming to bat was Babe Ruth.

Hubbell, it seemed, was in real trouble but what happened next has gone down in history as the most amazing pitching performance of all times. He struck out Babe Ruth, and then he struck out Lou Gehrig. In the next inning, he struck out Jimmie Foxx, Al Simmons and Joe Cronin. These men were five of the greatest hitters that ever played baseball. He struck them all out consecutively and he did it with the screwball.

Most pitchers don't throw the screwball anymore because it is a difficult pitch to throw and much more difficult to master. Nobody mastered it better than Carl Hubbell. The idea of the screwball is that it curves in the opposite direction of a normal curve ball. Carl Hubbell was left-handed. His curveball would normally break away from a left-handed hitter and into a right-handed hitter. The screwball on the other hand curves into a left-handed hitter and away from a right-handed hitter.

From 1935 till June 1946, the managers selected the entire All-Star team in each league. From 1947 to 1957, fans chose the team's starters and the manager chose the pitchers and remaining players. From 1958 through 1969, managers, players and coaches made all of the selections. From 1970 until the present day, fans make the selections. In 1933 there were eighteen nominees in each league. Today there are thirty-four nominees.

Starting in 1933 and well into the 1980's, most of the players nominated for the All-Star game played all, if not most of the entire game. After all, the fans voted to see the best players in baseball play not just a few innings, but the entire game. Today, (in 2011), with thirty teams in both leagues and thirty-four nominees, it is virtually impossible to have the players selected play more than a few innings before they have to be replaced by other players and it is quite a demanding task for the managers to try to get everyone played.

There were some memorable moments in All-Star game history and of course each game had its heroes. But in particular, a few highlights stand out: One we have already mentioned with Carl Hubbell striking out five of the greatest hitters in a row; the second was that there were three walk-off home runs. In the 1941 All-Star game, Ted Williams hit a walk-off home run off Claude Paseau of the Cubs; in 1955, Stan Musial performed the same feat off of Frank Sullivan and in 1964, Johnny Callison hit a walk-off home run off of Dick Radatz. Then in 1983, Fred Lynn of the Angels hit the first All-Star grand slam home run in history.

In the 1946 Mid-Summer Classic at Fenway Park in Boston, Ted Williams exhibited an incredible display of battling power. Nothing like it has been seen before or since. The first time up, Williams walked. The next two times at bat, he homered and singled against Kirby Higbe. His fourth time up, he singled off Ewell Blackwell and climaxed the day with a home run against Truett (Rip) Sewell with two out in the 8th inning. He had two home runs, two singles, and five runs batted in.

William's second homerun came off Sewell's celebrated blooper pitch. The pitch was nothing more than a soft lob that came to the plate in a high arc. No one had ever hit a homerun off of this pitch. When Williams came to bat, he tried to reach this pitch but missed. The next one came floating in and Ted Williams took two steps forward and hit it into the right field bleachers. "That was the greatest

one man batting show I have ever seen," recalls
Charlie Grimm who managed the losing National
Leaguers. (Reference: Baseball's Greatest Moments
by Joseph Reichler. Originally published in 1915
and updated in 1987 by Sammis Publishing
Company, copyrighted 1974 by Rutledge Books Inc.)

The way the All-Star game started in the height
of the Great Depression there is a strange paradox.
While the country was living in a state of poverty,
baseball was having its finest period; records were
established that have never been broken and some
of the greatest baseball players that ever lived played.
To list a few examples, some of which have already
been mentioned, in 1930 lefty Grove won 31 games
and lost 4. The year before, he won 28 and lost 5.
The St. Louis Cardinal's Gas House Gang was the
most audacious, hard drinking, hard talking and
hard playing team that has ever played baseball.
They were a spectacle to see with their antics on the
field and the quality of their play.

Then in 1937, 1938 and 1939, there were the
Bronx Bombers. The New York Yankees may be the
best team that has ever been assembled, the
cornerstone of which was Joe DiMaggio who hit in
56 straight games. After he was finally stopped, he
hit in 16 more straight games. Then there was Ted
Williams who in 1941 hit .406. These feats have
never been approached and certainly not surpassed
since that time.
President Roosevelt, in 1942 wrote a letter, "The
Green Letter," to the Commissioner of Baseball,

Kennesaw Mountain Landis. In this letter, he stated that he felt that baseball should continue during the war. He said that it would be good for the working people to have a time of relaxation away from the tension and woes of the war. The Commissioner agreed and baseball continued.

The quality of baseball certainly did reflect the fact that most of the great players had joined the Armed Forces. I can remember Bob Feller enlisting in the Navy the day after Pearl Harbor and spending the rest of the war as a gunner on a Navy ship. Remember Ted Williams lost five years of his career as a fighter pilot - the best years of a baseball player's life between age 27 to 32. They were not alone as many baseball players met the call of their country and we can be proud of them, as we are of everyone who served.

After the war, it took a long time, perhaps five years to get back to the quality of baseball that had been played before the war but there will never be a time in baseball in all the country's history that Americans could stand so proud.

From the time of the first All-Star game in 1933 until the beginning of the Second World War, baseball, including the All-Star game, could not have had a closer relationship. It was as if one needed the other one. It was a time where there was no competition. Baseball was the only thing that people could look forward to during the Great Depression for pleasure and comfort where there are was only misery and poverty.

In 1946 baseball began its long journey back to the quality that it had before the war. However, things were not the same as they were during the 30's. The war economy got the country out of the depression and people had more money to spend. There were manufacturers that were ready to provide the items people wanted to buy and/or its passions were beginning to change from a dependence on baseball to other needs and interests.

As mentioned earlier in this book, television changed people's choices. They were no longer dependent on baseball as their one source of entertainment. Now their choices were to include other sports, various programs on television and a multitude of other interests that were created by television. There is no question that baseball was still the center of sports interest, but now with the games of the National Football League and the National Basketball Association being televised many fans were lured away from the national pastime.

When Jackie Robinson, broke the color barrier in 1947, many of the Negro leagues that were so numerous throughout the country folded because people now had an opportunity to see their favorite black players in the big leagues. The same thing happened to the lower minor leagues and the players in class D, C and B which made up the bulk of the minor leagues. They simply could not compete with television and were forced out of business.

In 1957 the Brooklyn Dodgers and the New York Giants moved to Los Angeles and San Francisco and thus began the Western migration of relocation and expansion which increased the Major Leagues from 16 teams in 1933 to 30 teams in 1999. In 1961 the baseball season went from 154 games to 162 games. In addition thirty games were played in spring training bringing the total number of games to 192 in a season. That then introduced realignment in both leagues and a playoff system was inaugurated whereby each league was divided into three sections: East, Central and West, with one wild-card team playing for the opportunity to compete in the World Series. This added to the number of games.

In 1945, because of the war there was no All-Star game but in 1946 baseball and the All-Star game began again in earnest. The All-Star game had become an intricate part of our national pastime but in the years that followed the war our country changed and baseball changed. Expansion realignment, population changes and a variety of things already discussed in this book were occurring and baseball was affected by all of them.

It would be difficult to highlight the great moments in each All-Star game from 1946 to the present, but without question, as in any other baseball game, there were heroes and there were some that didn't play as well. There was every bit of excitement that there is in any other game and there were memorable times that have gone down in history.

In 1985, prior to the All-Star game, baseball introduced the Home Run Derby to generate fan interest. Certain selected powerful home run hitters were chosen by each league to represent them in it and they would enter into a playoff to see how many home runs each one could hit in a specific bracket to determine who the ultimate winner would be. Then they introduced what was called the celebrity softball game in which prominent celebrities; former great baseball players and people from all walks of life participated. The game took on a carnival atmosphere; however, some people enjoyed this type of activity.

In another effort to add to interest in the game, in 2003 the decision was made to award home field advantage in the World Series to the team from the league that won the All-Star game.

The All-Star game unfortunately has lost some of the luster and appeal that it once had. This is by no means the fault of the players but it does reflect the fact that there are now 30 teams, where initially, there were 16. The season has been extended from 154 games to 162 games and spring training has been extended to 30 games and then when you consider the playoff structure that now exists I think you will admit that it makes for a long season.

In my judgment the season was just too long. After all, they would be playing baseball from the end of February until the end of October. As a result the All-Star game began to be less attractive to the fans than it once was. In 1933, eighteen players in each league were nominated to play in the All-Star game. In 2011, thirty-four players were nominated to play in the All-Star game. It doesn't take a mathematician to figure out the difficulty that a manager has and trying to get each of those players entered into the game to satisfy the fans.

But are they really satisfying the fans? In 1933 and 1934 those players that were nominated, played the entire game because that's what the people wanted to see. In 2011, the fans expected the same thing but what they got was their favorite player coming to bat once or twice and then being taken out for a pinch-hitter so that the manager could get all of the players in the game.

Two years ago, someone dreamed up the idea that each of the 30 teams would have at least one player to represent that team in the All-Star game. The effort to get every player into the game has on occasion left managers with no reserves. The tied 2002 game was stopped without a winner after the 11th inning when both teams ran out of pitchers. This led to a rule allowing one player plus a catcher to reenter the game as an exception to the standard no-return rule of baseball.

I will let the reader determine the wisdom of this ruling bearing in mind that we call this game the All-Star game and expect all-stars not one player from Podunk being put in as a pinch runner so that his name might appear in the box score.

Unfortunately, a number of players in the 2011 All-Star Game did not report and many of them if they were candid would admit that because of the length of the season those four days were a welcomed time off. The ratings for the All-Star game just past were the lowest that they have ever been.

I am afraid that the All-Star Game, as some sportswriters suggest, is being relegated to that of the Pro-Bowl Game in football. Football has four summer training games and an eighteen game grueling football season, then an eight game play off season to determine who plays in the Super Bowl game. Players are selected for their great performances during the year and are elected to the Pro-Bowl squad. These talented players are given a week of vacation with their families in Hawaii where they play the Pro-Bowl game. To most people, this game is of no significance and it doesn't really matter who wins or loses. There's no question that the players are honored for what they've achieved during the prior season but the game itself is lackluster. I'm afraid that the All-Star game is headed for the same fate. I hope I am wrong.

CHAPTER

Is This The Same Game Your Fathers Watched?

The purpose of this book was to point out the changes that have taken place in Major League Baseball since 1947. Prior to that, baseball had a special place in the heart of America. It was our game, our national pastime. And yes, for many of us, it was a part of our way of life. Baseball, at that time, was special. It had a certain romance, and an ambiance that captured the spirit of America. The teams were *our* teams. The players were *our* players. They were bigger than life and we looked up to them in awe.

It was a time of no television. The only way you were able to see these players were to go to the ballpark. Baseball was *our* sport and we didn't have to share it with anyone. We talked about it at work and at the barbershops and in the bars and listened to it on the radio if we lived in a big city. We couldn't wait to get the morning paper to read the box scores of the previous day's games. We knew that our team would have the same players this year as it had last year. Maybe a player would be traded and replaced by another, but mostly the same players would be there next year. Everyone kept up with the pennant races to see who would win the American or National championship.

Baseball teams then were family owned; the Wrigley's with the Cubs, the Comiskey's with the White Sox, the Griffiths' with the Washington Senators, the Stoneham's with the Giants and many other family names. Today, with a few exceptions, Major League teams are owned by corporations or conglomerates: Disney, AOL, Time Warner, and The Chicago Tribune to name a few.

Baseball had little competition and filled America's appetite. Sports such as professional basketball and professional football did not become prominent for another twenty years. Television became influential in late 1959 and the early 60's. That is when everything changed. The old romance with baseball was over, but not because people still didn't love baseball. *Television* gave people unlimited choices, and not just for sports, but for any other interests they might have. The love affair that America had with baseball was a special time, but as America changed so did baseball. Is this the same game your fathers watched? The answer is no. The game your father watched just faded away into history.

We have entered into the modern era where baseball has become a billion-dollar plus business. The bottom line rules the decision-making. Players are shuffled around from one team to another, like pawns on a chessboard. The fans don't know from one year to the next, which players will be on their team and which will be on some other team. Everything has changed. We now have free agency. With the addition of post season playoffs, teams with the best win and loss record, may not even get to play in the World Series. We have the designated hitter (DH) rule in the American League. The same genius that figured out the 14/16 team arrangements may have initiated the DH rule. Who knows?

Many changes baseball organizers have made were beneficial for the game, such as: breaking the color barrier, expansion relocation and realignment, the destruction of the reserve clause and the players union. The changes in pitching philosophy, the pitch count and management decisions which are now based on computerized profiles of opposing players tendencies and percentages are all automated.

There is nothing wrong with that. It is just a stark contrast between the way it was and the way it is now. Winning is paramount and money wins games. The team with the most money can buy the best players and generally have the highest winning percentages. There are measures that baseball has taken to even up the situation, like revenue sharing. Revenue sharing is a procedure where all teams put a percentage of their gate receipts into a central pool. This pool is then distributed on a percentage basis to the least successful team and to the most successful team. The baseball draft is another way baseball tries to attain parity. The last place teams get to pick the highest draft choices and the top teams get lower draft choices. Though these

measures are useful, baseball has yet to solve the
money problem where teams with the most money,
like the New York Yankees, can afford to buy the
best players.

The Supreme Court's decision in 1922 said that
baseball was entertainment and does not come
under the Sherman antitrust laws as a monopoly.
This is a far cry from what Major League Baseball is
today. It all goes back to the inside page of this
book where it says, remember rule one. Rule one is
it all boils down to the money.

CHAPTER

Why Are Major League Batting and Power Averages Down?

Since 1947 when Jackie Robinson broke the color barrier to the present time there have been many important changes in major league baseball.

We are going through another important change that few readers and fans are completely aware of. This change has been going on for about 12 years. Batting averages, power averages including single, doubles, triples and home runs are all going down. The chart below shows the averages for the last 6 years and has been supplied by ESPN.Go.com.

Year	AVG	HITS	XBH	HR	SLG	STRIKE OUTS
2011	.255	1409	462	152	.399	1150
2010	.257	1418	470	158	.403	1144
2009	.262	1451	491	168	.418	1120
2008	.264	1466	493	163	.416	1096
2007	.268	1499	503	165	.422	1073
2006	.269	1502	517	180	.432	1055
DOWN	.014	93	55	28	.033	UP 95

These statistics show that major league teams are down in almost every category. Each team was down an average of 28 homeruns, 93 less hits and 95 more strikeouts then there were 6 years earlier.

According to fangraphs.com in the period of 2002-2005, only 19.3 hitters were swinging at balls out of the strike zone. In 2006 hitters swung at 23.5% of pitches outside the strike zone. This compares to 30% in 2011.Apparently the hitters were not able to follow the ball from the time it left the pitcher's hand to the time it entered the catcher's mitt.

Another startling statistic will get your attention. In the past 6 years including 4 games in 2012, there have been 26 no hit or perfect games pitched. In the prior 6 years there were only 7 no hit or perfect games pitched. Isn't that amazing?

From 1875, you read it right, until the year 2000 the average for no hit or perfect games were less than one per year. If a pitcher pitched a no hit game his picture would appear in every sport page in the country. If he pitched a perfect game he might get invited to the White House.

I think it would be fitting at this time to explain the difference between a no hit game and a perfect game. A no hit game is a game in which the pitcher or pitchers do not allow the other team to get a single, double, triple or home run/no hits. On the other hand, they may walk one or more batters. They could hit one or more batsman and get to 1st base that way. Another way to gain a base is when one of the pitcher's team mates commits an error or commits what is called catcher's interference. In this situation, as the batter swings at the ball the catcher hits or touches the bat and the batter is awarded first base. There is a fifth way that a batter can reach 1st base on a no hit game. On a swinging third strike, where the ball gets past the catcher, the batter may race to 1st base. If he reaches 1st base before the catcher throws him out, he is allowed to remain on 1st base.

In a perfect game the pitcher faces 27 batters and gets 27 outs. The results are no walks, no hit batsman and no errors by his team mates, no catcher interference or no swinging third strikes that allows the batsman 1st base.

In the long history of baseball there have been only 280 no hit games and 24 perfect games pitched. Included in those numbers were 3 no hit games in 2012 and 1 perfect game.

There are a number of theories why these averages are falling. One theory is that the hitters are swinging from their heels meaning they are swinging as hard as they can, hoping that the bat will make contact with the ball. Another theory is that modern players are taught to swing with their arms and not with their entire body.

From all of the statistical information we have, I have a completely different theory. One fact is very clear. The pitchers are dominating the hitters with their speed. There are 2 reasons for this:

One - We now have 30 teams with a rooster of 25 players per team or 750 players. If we exclude 11 pitchers from each team, that would bring us down to 450 players. I do not believe that there are 450 great baseball players in the whole world. There might not even be 300. In other words, the talent is stretched to thin. Look at the last 2 All Star games. You saw a lot of good ball players but you didn't see a lot of great ball players. I believe this is one reason that batting averages have gone down. My observation is too many teams and not enough talent.

Two – The 2nd part of my theory deals with the speed of the pitchers fast ball. On each major league roster of 25 players, the team carries between 11 – 12 pitchers. Each of these pitchers including the relief pitchers pitch balls between 91 - 95 miles per hour or higher.

When a batter sets up in the batters box he is ready to receive a 91 mph plus fast ball. As a result he must start his swing a little sooner. When he does this, his timing is changed and he might not follow the ball from the pitcher's hand into the catcher's mitt. If he gets something other than a fast ball, such as a hard breaking slider or a change of pace that starts at his knees and winds up in the dirt and he strikes at it. It increases the probability of striking out and swinging at balls outside of the strike zone.

Essentially it starts with the 91, 92, 93, 94 and 95 mph fast ball. The faster pitching affects the hitters reaction speed which results in more strike outs.

Baseball has thrown another road block in the hitter's path.

1. This is the shift system that is employed by certain teams against certain players. This all stems from the baseball statisticians that calculate that certain hitters have a greater tendency to hit the ball in certain places around the infield. The team in the field simply moves the second baseman and shortstop into those lanes where the hitter generally hits the ball. As a result, the balls are caught which cuts down the hitters batting average.

2. The out fielders gloves have changed. They now have elongated webbing in the gloves. Make no mistake the diving outfielders catches are truly amazing. Just to get to the ball boggles the mind. Most of these catches are made in the webbing of the glove and snared. In the older era the ball had to be caught in the pocket of the smaller glove. As a result many of these great catches today would not be made using the older gloves.

I think that the domination of pitching is a major change. The statistics bears this out. The result has already been seen. We now have lower scoring games

3-2, 4-3 etc... There is nothing basically wrong with that. It is just a change in the game.

Is there a solution to this growing trend? I do not see one in the foreseeable future. The pitchers are certainly not going to throw any slower. To adjust, the hitters will have to speed up their hitting.

So what can be done to help the hitters change this downward trend? Let a team, any team select 3 or 4 of their best regular players and have them meet with the best eye doctors that specializes in depth perception. They would go to a one month class and concentrate on watching the pitch released from the pitchers hand into the catchers mitt. This would be a concentrated program much like speed reading. These players would be rotated each month and then tested to see if this program increases their hitting ability.

This idea may have been tried by some teams. It is certainly an idea that is worth trying.

CHAPTER

Radio Announcers

It would be difficult to overestimate the impact that the local radio announcers have had on baseball. As discussed in other chapters, baseball was a major source of comfort to Americans doing the difficult days of the Great Depression. Only a small percentage of those living near one of the sixteen teams could attend a game with any degree of regularity, but nearly everyone had a radio.

Tuning in the games provided cost-free entertainment to people who could not afford to spend money on other forms of recreation, and housewives and youngsters at home (many a schoolboy or schoolgirl would rush home after classes to catch the game), unemployed men, and even many who were working managed to tune in the game.

As a result, they became rapid fans of one of the home teams; their children followed, and generations of families put the "fanatic" in "fan." The commitment to baseball on the radio that developed as radio grew in the 1930's continued on into the early 1940's, when the United States was engaged in World War II, which also resulted in great limitations on the availability of any other entertainment. When the war ended in 1945 and Americans found themselves with lots more discretionary income, they began to flock to the ballparks in large numbers, anxious to see in person the heroes for whom they cheered beside the radio speaker. This played a major part in the growth and expansion of baseball.

In those days, two or more teams in one city were common–three in New York, and two in each of Boston, Chicago, Philadelphia, and St Louis. Cincinnati, Cleveland, Detroit, Pittsburgh, and Washington were the one-team towns. In the five multiple team cities, the degree to which the announcer appealed to listeners often determine which team an individual rooted for. The following is a rundown of just some of the more popular announcers who contributed so much to America's love affair with baseball. They are not in any particular order, and no popularity ranking is intended. Each was immensely popular in his own city but some were little known beyond it.

Harry Caray is one of the best known announcers, primarily because, unlike most who were known only to those following one team, Caray, via cable television later became something of a legend all over the country. While Carey played semi-pro baseball for a short time, he got into radio at age 19 and spent the rest of his life as a broadcaster.

He handled basketball (the old St. Louis Hawks), football (University of Missouri and three Cotton Bowl games), then landed the job of St Louis Cardinals announcer in 1945 (he also covered St Louis Browns games initially, broadcasting only home games of each team (both could not play at home on the same day as they shared Sportsman's Park).

Carey covered the Cardinals for 25 years, through the 1969 season. After one season with the Oakland Athletics, he took over the Chicago White Sox radio booth in 1971. There he developed a reputation as quite a character, even broadcasting bare-chested from the bleachers. In 1981, Carey switched to the Chicago Cubs. Since the Cubs television station was available nationwide via cable, Carey developed into a legend across America, best known for getting on the public address system as well as TV and leading the fans in singing "Take Me Out To The Ball Game."

Carey remained with the Cubs until his death in 1998. So well regarded was he that the Cubs wore a caricature patch on their uniforms throughout the 1998 season, Sammy Sosa dedicated his 66 home runs to him, and a statue of Carey leading the singing stands outside Wrigley Field. He received numerous awards and honors.

Vin Scully holds the record for tenure, with an incredible 64 seasons and counting with the Brooklyn-turned Los Angeles Dodgers. No sports broadcaster in any sport comes close to his affiliation with a single team. He began as a student on the

Fordham University station. Later, he came to the attention of another legend, the Brooklyn Dodgers' Red Barber, who he joined in the Dodger booth in 1950. Scully became the lead announcer when Barber left in 1953, moved with them to Los Angeles in 1958, and has remained with them ever since. There he became so popular that fans would bring portable radios with them to the stadium to hear Scully call the game they were watching. In 1976, the fans voted him the "most memorable personality" in the history of the franchise.

Scully, too, is known beyond his broadcasting city due to wide exposure broadcasting playoff games as well as other sports and activities on network television. He, too, has received many awards and honors.

Mel Allen was known as the "Voice of the New York Yankees," After a short stint with the Washington Senators, Allen became the lead announcer for the New York Yankees and Giants in 1939, covering the home games of both teams. Perhaps the most memorable moment of his career was when a dying Lou Gehrig told him, that his broadcasts were the only thing that was keeping that baseball legend going. Allen kept his composure until Gehrig departed, then broke down in tears.

Allen entered the Army in 1943 (World War II) but returned to do Yankee broadcasts exclusively after the war, covering them on the road as well as at home. Because the Yankees were so often in the World Series (in those days the announcers for the two World Series teams were used for the network Series broadcasts), Allen, too, became widely known. He called 22 World Series and 24 All-Star games.

At the end of the 1964 season, the Yankees fired Allen–no reason was ever given–and fans were outraged. He worked Milwaukee Braves games in 1965 and for the Cleveland Indians in 1968. The Yankees rehired him in 1976 and he remained with them until 1985. He was given many awards and honors, and the Yankees put a plaque for him in Yankee Stadium, calling him a Yankee institution and a national treasure.

Few announcers were as well-known as Jay Hanna "Dizzy" Dean. Needless to say, the fact that he's in baseball's Hall of Fame as one of the game's finest pitchers helps (he's one of only two pitchers in the last 78 years to win 30 games in a season).

After retiring as a pitcher in 1941, Dean took to the radio booth for the St Louis Cardinals (1941-46), St Louis Browns (1941-48), Yankees (1950-51) and Atlanta Braves (1966-68). He also did network broadcasts for Mutual (1952), ABC (1953-54) and CBS (1955-1965). He was best known as a colorful character who employed grammatically incorrect English. He too received his share of awards and honors, including a post office named after him by act of Congress.

Ernie Harwell spent 42 of his 55 years in baseball broadcasting with the Detroit Tigers and is best known for his connection to that team. He is unique, though, in that he's the only announcer whoever was traded for a player. While broadcasting minor league games in Atlanta in 1948, he was traded for a catcher so that he could provide an emergency replacement for Brooklyn's famous Red Barber, who had been hospitalized.

He remained with Brooklyn through 1949, then went to the New York Giants from 1950 to 1953, Baltimore Orioles 1954-1959, before becoming the voice of the Tigers in 1960, where he teamed with Harry Carey's son, Paul from 1973 to 1991. He was fired at the end of that season, bringing a firestorm of criticism down on the Tigers and the radio station.

After working for the California Angels in 1992, new Tiger management made it a priority to bring Harwell back to Detroit, where he continued from 1993 to 2002, when he retired. Less well known beyond his core city than some of the other announcers, Harwell did broadcast on network two All-Star games and two World Series, along with other playoff series and CBS' Game of the Week. Engaged in a variety of other activities as well as baseball, Harwell earned many awards. He died in 2010, lay in repose in the Tigers stadium where over 10,000 fans filed past his casket, a flag with his initials was hoisted in center field, and the Tigers wore a commemorative patch on their uniforms that season.

Phil Rizzuto is another baseball Hall of Famer who went on to an equally stellar career in announcing, calling Yankee games for 40 years. He began in 1957, following his last season as a player and continued through1996. All together he spent most of seven decades in the Yankee organization, as a minor then major league player and broadcaster. His number 10 has been retired, he has a plaque in Yankee Stadium's Monument Park, and has a park named for him in Union, New Jersey.

Few announcers covered as many sports as Jack Buck but still became known for their identification with one team. Buck covered a lot of football, hockey, basketball, wrestling, boxing, and bowling, while also calling St Louis Cardinal games from 1954 to 2000. During that time, he covered 11 World Series, 18 Super Bowls, and four All-Star games.

Many people who had occasion to hear several of these men calling baseball consider Buck to be the best of all time. He was known best for his distinctive play-by-play calls and his deep, gravelly voice. During his almost half a century as the voice of the Cardinals, he covered such baseball greats as Stan Musial, Lou Brock, and Bob Gibson. He called Mark McGuire's record-breaking 70th home run and Kirk Gibson's "unbelievable" home run in the first games of the 1988 World Series.

After three years covering Cardinal minor league farm teams, Buck was promoted to the Cardinals in 1954, dropped in 1959, but hired again in 1961. He was teamed with Harry Caray for ten years and became the lead play-by-play announcer when Carey left. Buck passed away in 2002, a victim of lung cancer and Parkinson's disease. He was well respected in St. Louis, where he regularly volunteered time to host charity events, and within two hours of his death, people were leaving flowers at the base of his bust outside Busch Stadium, even though it was the middle of the night. Flags were lowered to half-staff, and local TV anchors all wore black suits for several days. A public visitation was held in the stadium, and thousands filed past his coffin. Among many honors, Jack Buck was inducted into the Radio Hall of fame in 1995.

Curt Gowdy also covered many nationally televised sporting events but was best known for his long stint as the voice of the Boston Red Sox. After working with Mel Allen for the New York Yankees in 1949-50, Gowdy went to the Red Sox in 1951 and remained for 15 years, until 1965 (missing the 1957 season due to health problems). Later, he worked for ABC CBS, and NBC, covering so many sports that he earned the nickname, the "broadcaster of everything." He covered 13 World Series, 16 All-Star games, 9 Super Bowls, 14 Rose Bowls, 8 Olympics, and 24 NCAA Final Fours. He is in 22 Halls of Fame and has a state park in Wyoming named for him.

Russ Hodges launched himself into baseball broadcasting immortality with his famous call of Bobby Thompson's pennant winning home run for the New York Giants in 1951–"the Giants win the pennant, the Giants win the pennant, the Giants win the pennant...!!!!!!" Hodges began with the Washington Senators in 1941 and worked for the Chicago Cubs, Chicago White Sox, Cincinnati Red, New York Yankees and New York Giants. He became lead announcer for the Giants after they split off their radio network from the Yankees in 1949 and began covering road as well as home games. He remained with the Giants for the next 22 seasons, both in New York and San Francisco.

Bob Prince was known primarily in Pittsburgh, where he broadcast Pirate games for 28 years, from 1948 to 1975. He did get prominence outside his home city, though, when, on a dare from a Pirate player, he jumped from the third floor of a St Louis hotel into a swimming pool. Nicknamed "The Gunner" he became a part of the culture in Pittsburgh. He broadcast three World Series (two because Pittsburgh was in it) and one All-Star game.

After a change in broadcasting management, Prince was fired in 1975, and, like the removals of popular announcers in other cities, the Pirate fans reacted violently. There was a parade and downtown rally for him, and several Pirate players also spoke up in his behalf. Prince went to the Houston Astros for one year and dabbled in other efforts until he was rehired in 1985. However, he was battling cancer by that time and could only announce a few home games before passing away in June of that year.

Red Barber "The Ol' Redhead," was an institution in the New York area from 1939 to 1966. His entry into broadcasting was indeed unusual–enrolled in the University of Florida and working as a janitor to pay his way, he was pulled from his janitorial duties to fill in behind the University microphone as an emergency replacement when a scheduled professor failed to show up. The experience caused him to switch careers from education to broadcasting.

Hired by the Cincinnati Reds in 1934, he called the first major league game he had ever seen. He remained with the Red through 1938, then called Brooklyn Dodger games from 1939 to 1953 and New York Yankee games with Mel Allen, 1954-1966. He covered football in the New York area as well. Known for his folksy style (e.g. "The bases are F.O.B. (full of Brooklyns)", Barber retired in 1966 after being dismissed by the Yankees. The recipient of many awards, Barber was in the inaugural class of the American Sportscasters Association Hall of Fame, joining some of the most illustrious names in sports casting.

Jack Brickhouse was Harry Carey's predecessor with the Chicago Cubs, covering that team from 1948 to 1981. He also called White Sox games until 1968, as each team broadcast only their home games until that time. In his time, he was as well-known on Chicago's north side as was Carey in his tenure. Brickhouse covered three World Series, a Rose Bowl, and two NFL Championship Games, along with wrestling, boxing, and Chicago Bears football. He served in the Marine Corps during World War II and missed the only time in his long tenure that the Cubs won the pennant (1945).

Bob Murphy broadcast New York Mets games from the team's inception in 1962 until his retirement in 2003. Previously, he worked the

Boston Red Sox in 1954 and the Baltimore Orioles in 1960. Altogether, he spent 50 years doing major league play-by-play, broadcasting from every stadium in the National League. Murphy also called football, hockey, and bowling. A member of the Baseball Hall of Fame, Murphy was honored after his death in 2004 by a patch on the sleeves of the Mets uniforms.

In Philadelphia, the cultural icon was Harry Halas, who covered Phillies games from 1971 until his death at the beginning of the 2009 season. Although he succeeded a popular broadcaster, Bill Campbell, he quickly won the hearts of the Phillies fans. Halas covered six no-hit games, six National League Championship Series, three World Series, and both the first and the last game at Veterans Stadium and first at Citizens Bank Park. He teamed with former Phillies star Richie Ashburn for 27 seasons, and both were beloved figures in Philadelphia. He was posthumously inducted into the National Radio Hall of Fame, and a statue of him has been placed in Citizens Bank Park.

While far less known, Spanish language broadcaster Felo Ramírez is worthy of mention (as are several others had space allowed). The Spanish language radio voice of the Miami Marlins, he also has been broadcasting boxing since 1948. Born in Bayamo, Cuba, he is known as *"El Orgullo de Bayamo"* ("The Pride of Bayamo") by many who follow him. In 2001, he received the Ford C. Frick Award from the National Baseball Hall of Fame.

We are now living in the television age. Baseball is now delivered to us not only by sound but also by sight for our added enjoyment. We now have 30 teams instead of 16. Each broadcaster has one or more analyst or color man in the booth with him. He does the play by play and they analyze what we are seeing. In the old era the radio announcer gave us every aspect of the game in his own special way.

With a few exceptions they are all gone, but those of us who remember them including our fathers and mothers will always remember this group of men who enriched our lives.

ADDENDUM

The 1932 World Series, "the Babe Calls His Shot"

It has been 78 years since the 1932 World Series and the argument still persists whether or not Babe Ruth extended his arm and pointed to the right center field bleachers before hitting a long home run off of Charlie Root. I am going to tell you the story of that game, and then I'm going to tell you the truth about what really happened, and hopefully we can put the argument and the controversy to rest once and for all.

Even before the series started, there was bad blood between the two teams. The Cubs bought Mark Koning from the Detroit Tiger's on April 25, 1932. Koning had been a regular player with the New York Yankees before that. He only played 33 games because of injuries. He did not play in the World Series. At that time and still as it is today, the players share in a portion of the gate receipts of the first four games of the World Series. In 1932, 60% of the total gate receipts went into a pool, 36.96% went to the winning team and 24.9% went to the losing team.

Babe Ruth

Charlie Root

When it is determined that a team is going to go
into the World Series, there is a closed door meeting
held for players only to determine to whom the
shares will be awarded. For example, all of the
regular players would receive a full share, the
coaches may receive a full share, and the trainer
may receive a full share. The clubhouse man may
receive a half of share. In 1932, the amount that
went to the winners was $5231.75 and the losers
received $4244.60. Because Koning had only played
33 games, the Cubs awarded him a one half share.
Being a favorite with the Yankee players, this
enraged the entire ball club against the Cubs.

At that time, there was an unwritten rule called
the non-fraternization principle. No player dared to
have any friendly conversation with anyone on the
other team or he would receive of verbal flogging
from the manager and the players. The other team
was the enemy and you were there to beat them
any way that you could, which generally included
calling the other players every vile name that could
be thought of. Babe Ruth was the perfect target for
the Cubs abuse because he loved to take it, but he
enjoyed giving it back as well.

In addition to the non fraternization rule, most
players at that time were uneducated and came from
blue collar families or from farms. Most of them,
but not all, drank and were hard living, hard talking
tough guys. But for all their personal failings, they
had one thing in common. They were all very good
baseball players. During this World Series, the

bench jockeys were in full swing calling each other names. In the fifth inning of the third game, Babe, came to bat and Charlie Root, threw him an inside fastball for a strike. The next pitch was a ball and as the benches jeered each other, Babe, put up two fingers signaling that he had two strikes left.

The next pitch was called a strike on the outside corner and Babe extended one finger indicating that he had one strike left. Charlie then threw him a curve ball. He hit it over the right center field bleachers in Wrigley Field. All the sports writers including Grantland Rice, who was at that time the dean of sports writers in the country, said that because Ruth extended one finger, he actually indicated that he was going to hit the next ball out of the ballpark. When the sports writers asked the Babe if he actually pointed he said, and I quote, "It's in the paper; read the paper". He never claimed that he actually pointed. Old film footage indicates that Ruth had never pointed and several years later at a private film showing, it was seen that Ruth did not point and Charlie Root was vindicated. In 1942, Charlie Root and Babe Ruth met at the filming of the Yankees about Lou Gehrig and Charlie asked him, "Did you point?" Babe said, "No, but it made a hell of a story."

Now I am going to tell you why I know that what I have just described to you is absolutely true. In 1950, I was playing for the Des Moines Cubs in the class A Western league. My manager was Charlie Root. We had just finished an eight-game series, four in Colorado Springs and four in Denver and were coming back on the train. Four of us, had turned the seats around so they were facing each other, and we had a small table between us and we were playing pinochle. We also had a small radio on the table.

At that time there were no broadcasts of Major League Baseball games unless you lived in a big city and your team was playing that day. What a radio station did was to broadcast simulated games. These were games in which the announcers would read the play-by-play description of the game, and have the crowd noises piped in, and when they did, it was difficult to distinguish that this was not an actual game being broadcast.

Charlie Root, was sitting right behind us when the game was going on. The particular game that they chose to broadcast that day was from the 1932 World Series—it was the Babe-calls-his-shot game. When Charlie heard the start of this game, he leapt out of his seat and came around and said, "Turn that blank, blank thing off, or I'll throw it out of the window." Charlie was a rough guy that nobody was going to mess with.

After he calmed down some, Charlie told us exactly what had happened in that 1932 series. He repeated essentially all that I have previously written, but added "If that big gorilla had pointed, I would have stuck one in his ear". He said it never happened and the Babe never extended his arm and pointed to the right center field.

In 1948, Hollywood produced the Babe Ruth story starring William Bendix. It was a complete flop. Prior to that, they had contacted Charlie and offered him $5000 to appear in that movie. He refused. And I can tell you with absolute certainty that Charlie Root went to his grave denying that this ever happened with Babe Ruth. I believe that I am the oldest man in the United States that knows the truth about this story because I played for the man who threw the pitch to Babe Ruth.

ABOUT THE AUTHOR

Jim Forbes was born January 15, 1927 in Chicago, Illinois. He was educated in Chicago's public schools and went through the great depression. Prior to his graduation from high school, he signed a minor league contract with the Chicago Cubs. Upon graduation in June of 1945, he was inducted into the Army Air Corp and served in the army of occupation in Germany in 1945 and 1946. He was honorably discharged in January of 1947. In March of that year, he began his 7 year minor league career with the Marion Ohio Cubs Class D baseball. In 1949 he was brought to Wrigley Field to try out for the Chicago Cubs as a non roster player. Although that did not work out, it did not keep Jim from going as far as he could in the minor league Cub system. In 1951, he was elevated to Springfield, Ma. Class Triple A baseball of the International League. He played against Tommy Lasorda who then played for Montreal and would become the future manager of the Los Angeles Dodgers. In 1954, Jim had the opportunity of managing Deland in the Florida State League.

In the winter of 1950, Jim decided to continue his education using the GI Bill. Stetson University in Deland Florida was on the quarter system which made it possible for Jim to play baseball and still go to college. Jim graduated from Stetson University in 1954. During his 4 years at Stetson, he assisted in the coaching of the Stetson University Baseball team.

After a 52 year career in the insurance business, Jim retired and resides with his wife, Nancy, in Orlando, Florida.